NATASHA CRELLIN

PRIMARY EARLY YEARS IN ACTION

IN ACTION SERIES

A **WALKTHRUs** PRODUCTION

hachette LEARNING

hachette LEARNING

www.hachettelearning.com

Together we unlock every learner's unique potential

At Hachette Learning (formerly Hodder Education), there's one thing we're certain about. No two students learn the same way. That's why our approach to teaching begins by recognising the needs of individuals first.

Our mission is to allow every learner to fulfil their unique potential by empowering those who teach them. From our expert teaching and learning resources to our digital educational tools that make learning easier and more accessible for all, we provide solutions designed to maximise the impact of learning for every teacher, parent and student.

Aligned to our parent company, Hachette Livre, founded in 1826, we pride ourselves on being a learning solutions provider with a global footprint.

To order, please visit www.HachetteLearning.com or contact Customer Service at education@hachette.co.uk / +44 (0)1235 827827.

ISBN: 978 1 9152 6177 9

First published in 2026 by
Hachette Learning (a trading division of Hodder & Stoughton Limited),
An Hachette UK Company
Carmelite House
50 Victoria Embankment
London EC4Y 0DZ
www.HachetteLearning.com

The authorised representative in the EEA is Hachette Ireland, 8 Castlecourt Centre, Dublin 15, D15 XTP3, Ireland (email: info@hbgi.ie)

Impression number 10 9 8 7 6 5 4 3 2 1
Year 2030 2029 2028 2027 2026

Illustrations by DC Graphic Design Limited, Hextable, Kent.
Typeset in the UK.
Printed in the UK.

A catalogue record for this title is available from the British Library.

EDITOR INTRODUCTION

At the time of writing, our Early Years Foundation Stage (EYFS) classrooms contain the 'Covid babies' – those children born during a national lockdown and whose early childhood experiences have been like those of no other generation before. These children's experiences of EYFS are, therefore, even more important as a result of the disruption to, and difference in, their early lives and pre-school experiences. In *Primary Early Years in Action*, Natasha has managed to capture not only the importance of EYFS but also to precis the practical and narrate the how and the why. Drawing on decades of experience in the phase, Natasha has outlined the key considerations for anyone working with our youngest children and in developing an effective setting. Whether you are an experienced EYFS practitioner, new to the phase or a school leader who wants to know more about exemplifying and developing best practice, this *In Action* book provides an excellent prompt and tool for discussion, review and action.

Working with our youngest children in school as we welcome them into formal education is a joy and a unique one. Our youngest learners are not simply big kids in small bodies; they require a specialist and thoughtful approach, rooted in play and fired by a deep understanding of child development alongside joy, nurture and humour. Children's early experiences are so influential and integral to their future happiness and success that it is imperative that we get this right. *Primary Early Years in Action* has been a delight to read and edit and I know it will be an indispensable guide for thinking about your provision and the privilege it is to play and grow alongside our little learners. As Ralph Waldo Emerson said,

> *'It is a happy talent to know how to play.'*

CONTENTS

CHAPTER 1
THE BIG PICTURE

Many teachers who teach in early years do so because they have always wanted to work in this phase. However, many teachers who find themselves in early years have had no formal training in early years pedagogy or practice. At some time in their career, they have been approached by the headteacher, encouraging them to have a go at teaching in the nursery or in Reception. This move is exciting, but the leap from National Curriculum to early years can be overwhelming. Knowing where to start, and being confident assessing when things are going well (or badly), is difficult at first. To add to this, in many schools there is only one early years teacher, meaning there is no one to share problems with or get advice from. This book aims to help you on your journey when everything feels new and you can't see the wood for the trees.

This book is not theoretical. It is about the practical applications of running an effective early years class. It describes the essential components, and acts as a starting point. This book can be a springboard into accessing additional books, some with more complex explorations of theory, pedagogy and research.

The philosophy and approach to teaching in early years are different to those in other year groups. Understanding why things are done as they are may be tricky for those who are new to teaching young children. This book aims to support your understanding and give guidance as to where to start and what to focus on.

Early years education covers the age ranges from birth to 5 years of age. The first five years of a child's life will see them develop from a vulnerable baby, completely dependent on adults for all aspects of survival, to being able to speak in complex sentences, write sentences, read, move in multiple ways, ride a bike, be able to hold and maintain relationships, and understand complex social norms and expectations. The brain has grown to 90% of its final size by the time a child is five. No other teacher will see such incredible development in the children in their class, and this is what makes teaching young children so exciting and rewarding. Children's experiences and interactions during early childhood are pivotal in their development, and the quality of the teaching they receive at this age has a tremendous impact.

There are unique challenges to teaching young children that are more easily mitigated with older children. The most obvious is attention span, and the ability to concentrate for long on a task. Young children are constantly moving both physically and in their interests. What absorbs them one day may be different the next. This is why planning is challenging, as even the most inspiring planning may not result in child engagement. It is these challenges that lead to some unique pedagogical approaches in early years.

Knowing where to start depends very much on the following:

- What is the quality of the provision you have just inherited? Is it strong or does it need rejuvenation?
- What is the profile of staff in the provision? Are they experienced early years practitioners who can support your journey or are they looking at you to take the lead?
- What is the headteacher's view of early years and how is this reflected in the school values and culture, on the school website and in documentation such as the School Improvement Plan?

If you are in a position where the setting needs radical overhaul, the staff are not experienced in early years and the senior leadership team (SLT) are not invested in early years, then this may be very challenging. However, if some of the other elements mentioned above are in a strong position, this will provide you with additional time to read and immerse yourself in early years literature and research, and to develop your skills and knowledge at a more comfortable pace.

Where to start:

1. **Find a mentor.** This could be a friend, family member or professional who is experienced and passionate about early years. Pick their brains whenever you can. Make links to other schools and join networks if you can. These people will become your source of information and inspiration. The early years community is a close knit and supportive one. Join the crowd and absorb from more-experienced colleagues.
2. **Understand the elements of this book.** Get comfortable with these ideas and make sure they are evident in your classroom. Each new topic in this book starts with a **key takeaways** section. This is a summary of the key areas that will be discussed in the section. Use this to remind you of the key points or to help you decide if you need to read further.

3. **Expand your knowledge.** Pick from the relevant areas in the other chapters of this book and elsewhere.

Early years has its own vocabulary and different terms can often mean the same thing, which may initially cause some confusion. Refer to the extra resources at the end of this book where you can find a glossary of the terms you may come across in early years and a brief description of what they mean.

CHAPTER 2
CORE CONCEPTS

This chapter considers the areas you need to understand to manage an effective early years classroom. If you can master each of the subheadings covered in this chapter, you will be well on your way to delivering strong provision, that supports, nurtures and educates the children in your care.

Child development

Key takeaways

- An overview of key knowledge of child development will help you to know how to meet the needs of learners at different stages of their development.
- Teaching should be aimed at the correct stage, not age, of development.
- Young children will learn best through play, taking advantage of hands-on experiences.

Unless you have trained as an early years teacher, it is unlikely that you have done any study on child development. Understanding child development from birth to five years is essential as it helps you to know where learners have come from, and the pathway you can expect them to follow. This knowledge is helpful when supporting children working above or below the age-expected range, including those with special educational needs and disabilities (SEND), or those that have had deprived early childhood experiences.

Child development is a large topic that cannot be fully addressed in the confines of any single book. Anyone teaching in early years should ensure that learning about child development is an integral part of their Continuing Professional Development (CPD) and proactively develop their knowledge on this subject. There is a great deal of information on the internet, and there are many free courses. An example is a free course offered on the Department for Education (DfE) site, which is worth taking some time to explore.

https://child-development-training.education.gov.uk/

The following is a brief summary of some of the information you should know about child development. The summary has been broken down into four areas of development, and all are equally important. Each of these areas will intersect and it is important not to lose sight of the whole child.

Age	Physical development	Communication and language development	Social and emotional development	Cognitive development
0–12 months	• Turns towards sounds • Interested in observing the environment • Can roll over and sit up without support • Can pull to standing • Crawls	• Babbles • Imitates sounds • Laughs • Uses some gestures, such as pointing	• Smiles • Enjoys playing with people • Wary of strangers • Close bond with familiar people • Expresses range of emotions	• Looks at things • Responds to others
1–2 years	• Walks • Stands alone • Drinks from a cup • Helps with dressing • Eats with a spoon • Jumps • Throws balls • Climbs • Dances	• Knows several words • Can follow simple instructions	• Plays simple pretend games • Expresses strong emotions, such as having tantrums	• Identifies by pointing to body parts • Interested in how objects work • Enjoys songs and music • Enjoys stories • Scribbles ➜

Age	Physical development	Communication and language development	Social and emotional development	Cognitive development
2–3 years	• Walks downstairs one foot at a time • Catches a ball • Goes down a slide • Turns lids and door knobs • Rides a tricycle • Turns individual pages of a book • Develops bowel and bladder control • Dresses and undresses • Can run well • Climbs on play structures	• Asks simple questions • Can name things • Uses two-word phrases • Says names of familiar people • Names pictures • Says 200–300 words	• Plays alongside other children and occasionally with them • Shows defiance	• Builds towers with blocks • Can follow a two-part instruction • Can group similar items by one category • Understands possession (i.e. 'This is mine') →

Age	Physical development	Communication and language development	Social and emotional development	Cognitive development
3–5 years	• Walks backwards • Climbs stairs confidently • Hops • Uses scissors • Propels on a swing • Goes to the toilet • Rides a tricycle and balance bike	• Can talk about their day • Speaks in sentences • Can answer a question about a story • Recites rhymes and songs • Understands that print has meaning	• Can play games with friends • Can engage in longer, imaginative play • Developing the concept of sharing • Developing more control over emotions	• Can do simple puzzles • Can draw simple figures • Knows numbers and colours • Can copy letters, numbers and simple shapes • Knows many phonemes and can read simple words • Can read and write first name • Can count out 10 objects • Understands past tense (yesterday) • Understands prepositions (on, under, behind) and pronouns (me, I, you)

Government curriculum documents will provide detail about the expectations for learning and development for each age group. Links to the documentation used in different parts of the United Kingdom are provided at the top of page 8.

The Birth to 5 Matters document published by Early Education on behalf of the Early Years Coalition and Early Education: https://birthto5matters.org.uk/

Development Matters: https://www.gov.uk/government/publications/development-matters--2

National practice guidance for early years in Scotland: https://education.gov.scot/resources/realising-the-ambition/

The Curriculum for Excellence Benchmarks (Scotland): https://education.gov.scot/curriculum-for-excellence/curriculum-for-excellence-benchmarks/

The Curriculum for Wales Progression Code: https://www.gov.wales/sites/default/files/publications/2021-11/curriculum-for-wales-progression-code.pdf

Make sure you understand the document used in your locality and refer to it frequently.

Key theorists and classroom application

Key takeaway

- Having an overview of the influential theorists will help you to understand why early years pedagogy is different from other school phases.

The first thing you notice as you look around an early years classroom is how different it looks to other classrooms. There are few desks, a lot of resources at child height and different learning spaces sectioned into zones. You will see unique resources to reflect the play-based approach to learning. For example, you are likely to see water trays, construction areas, snack tables, art areas and builders' tables. Spaces, such as the carpet area, are used more flexibly compared with other classrooms, and children use these spaces in a fluid way. The environment is central to all aspects of learning in early years and is carefully constructed. The design and approach have been influenced by many years of research and theory, with influencers dating from as early as the nineteenth century.

There are many early years texts that focus on theories and theorists who have influenced the development of early years pedagogy. You do not need to understand these in great depth to run a successful early years classroom. However, understanding how they have influenced good practice will help you to know why things are done the way they are, and to reflect on how they can be developed and improved. The following is a brief overview of some of the key theorists who have shaped early years education.

Froebel (1782–1852)

Key ideas	Impact on the classroom
Friedrich Froebel was the inventor of kindergartens. He described play as the highest expression of human development and identified the importance of children taking the lead in play, with the role of the adult to create an environment that supported and developed play. Froebel's ideas are evident in most early years curriculums, with a heavy emphasis on the value of play and the importance of a well-planned and resourced learning environment. Froebel highlighted the importance of using the senses when learning. Froebel felt children needed opportunities to make their own decisions and choices as this supports their self-regulation development. Froebel believed in the whole child and would not have supported a narrow curriculum. He identified concepts in learning as linked, rather than compartmentalised. Froebel's work has been used to construct the Froebelian principles.	Specific areas or zones of learning allow different types of play. Some examples of areas you may have in the classroom include: • block play • open-ended, loose-parts play • indoor/outdoor play • reading/book areas • mark-making areas • large physical play areas • musical and performance areas • small-world play areas • water play • natural items to explore • sensory areas. Learning opportunities should support senses (visual, hearing, touch). Young children need to be doing when learning, not just sitting and listening. Children need to face challenges in their learning that allow them to fail and struggle. This helps with the development of problem-solving skills and resilience, and an understanding of how to negotiate and how to ask for help. A strong range of emotional responses are important for young children and should not be seen as a negative thing. Children should be offered opportunities to make decisions on how and what they play. Overt adult control will not support this. Children should be allowed to play the same game, or with the same resources, repeatedly, to develop mastery and have the freedom to explore their own ideas. All aspects of a child's development should be a focus of early years education and a curriculum should be balanced to reflect this.

Steiner (1861–1925)

Key ideas	Impact on the classroom
Steiner philosophy had a focus on the use of open-ended resources. Children can use the resources in different ways dependent on their imagination. Rudolf Steiner believed the first seven years of life are critical to future life, with the first three years being the most important. A child's physical development is considered equal to the development of the spirit and soul. The rhythm of life is a focus in Steiner education, and a predictable pattern to the day is considered important.	When buying resources, try and look for things that can be used in multiple ways, such as blocks or planks. Avoid single-use toys if possible. The value and importance of the early years cannot be underestimated. This is the area where children will make most progress. Children need space both indoors and outdoors, and opportunities to move and develop their bodies. A dependable daily routine is important for children to feel secure. Having visual timetables and giving children time to discuss the day and expectations support this.

Montessori (1870–1952)

Key ideas	Impact on the classroom
Maria Montessori was one of the first to identify the ages 0–5 as being a special and important stage of development. She observed children playing with materials spontaneously and identified how the child and the environment interact together. She highlighted that the adult could support this interaction through careful support of the environment.	Children should be able to access areas of the learning environment freely – not needing adults to pass them things. This means resources should be within reach, and light enough for children to access, e.g. containers should not be so full that children cannot lift them from shelves. Furniture should be child sized to allow children comfort and support when exploring resources. Furniture should support independence.
The environment should be natural to avoid overstimulation and distraction. This means children can maintain focus on what they are learning from, rather than be distracted by decoration.	Where possible, the learning environment should be natural rather than bright and overstimulating. There should be a reduced number of resources available to allow items to be easily seen, such as 10 coloured pencils (rather than 50) or two pairs of scissors (rather than 30).
Soft furnishings allow for the transition from home to school.	Familiar items such as cushions, sofas, curtains and rugs will offer children a feeling of security, as they recognise these items and know how to use them.
Natural items support sensory experiences.	A variety of natural items, such as shells, pinecones and stones, will engage children's sensory learning.
Montessori discussed the spiritual environment as being important – this encompasses ideas of self-discipline, respectful engagement and inner strength of character. Cycles of activity are important in Montessori play. This includes choosing an activity and moving it to an appropriate workstation, using the materials, returning it to its original state for the next user, and then putting it away.	The tidy-up routine is an important part of the cycle of the day, and all children need to take part in this activity. Reinforce that children should not move on to a new activity until the one they have finished with has been put away. Strive to develop children's independence with activities like mealtimes. Children can be encouraged to pour their own drinks, get their own utensils and clear up plates.

Isaacs (1885–1948)

Key ideas	Impact on the classroom
Susan Isaacs believed that nursery education should be the normal experience for all young children. Isaacs believed that all parts of the environment and all resources should be carefully evaluated and planned for their impact on learning. The role of the practitioner in supporting learning is essential. Nursery was seen as an extension of home learning, and warmth and caring are essential elements of early years settings. Play is considered essential to learning. Children should be given responsibility for caring for the environment and should play an active part in cleaning it up and presenting it to a high standard.	Nursery and Reception provision should be a universal entitlement for all children. While this is the case with funded nursery places in the UK, not all children attending Reception classes have had this experience. All aspects of the environment should be carefully planned. Resources should be high quality. A nurturing culture is essential. A large percentage of the day should be play based. Children should be given tasks to complete to support classroom maintenance. Encourage children to wipe tables, pour milk, help wash up and sweep the floor as part of the daily routine. Provide them with appropriate-size brooms, dustpans and brushes, and cloths.

Piaget (1896–1980)

Key ideas	Impact on the classroom
Jean Piaget described four stages of cognitive development: • Sensorimotor stage (0–2 years) • Preoperational stage (2–7 years) • Concrete operational stage (7–11 years) • Formal operational stage (11 years through to adulthood). The stages most likely seen in early years are sensorimotor and preoperational. Sensorimotor stage – in this stage, children learn through their senses. They search for information that satisfies sensory needs and this may be done repeatedly. They may aim to achieve a goal, such as push buttons to make the light flash. Children in this stage begin to understand that objects exist and events happen independent of their own actions. This is called object permanence. Preoperational stage – children start to be able to understand abstract ideas and concepts. This can be seen in play, such as small-world play and dressing up – pretending an object is something else. Children start to categorise items and to develop a concept of number. Children are developing abstract ideas but still struggle to use logic, transform ideas or combine ideas. Children in this stage tend to focus on only one situation at a time and cannot see a situation from another's point of view, and hence are egocentric. Children will play alongside other children at the start of this stage and then begin to play with them as their understanding of others being separate to themselves develops.	Using the stages of development, most children in early years will be working in the sensorimotor and preoperational stages. This means: • Children need opportunities to do the same activity repeatedly. • Children need resources that focus on senses – items that are soft, rubbery, noisy things that can be pushed, pulled and manipulated. • Young children should not be forced to share as this is conceptually very difficult for children to do. There should be enough resources and enough space for children to engage in their own activities. However, adults should model the concept of sharing and discuss this concept within play. • Young children need to have opportunities to engage in small-world play and role play. • Children need to be immersed in number activities, such as songs and using hands-on items for counting. • Adults need to understand the limitations of these phases and to plan activities that reflect these phases.

Bourdieu (1930–2002)

Key ideas	Impact on the classroom
Pierre Bourdieu introduced the concept of 'cultural capital'. This is a theory that children's learning will be heavily influenced by the prior experiences they have had. The familiarity between the learning environment and their home culture will have an impact on how well children will settle into school. Bourdieu identified that many routines and expectations of school life are very different to the experiences of some children. An example of this is access to books, and immersion in traditional and well-known stories. Assumptions are made that children entering school have a knowledge of nursery rhymes, and work planned may reflect this assumption. This puts all the children for whom English is a second language, and children who have not had these experiences at home, at a disadvantage. This means children who do not share the cultural capital of the educational setting will be at a disadvantage before they even start learning.	Do not make assumptions that all children have had the same experiences before starting school. Look closely at vocabulary in books and stories. Do not assume all children have heard the words before, or that the vocabulary is understood, such as the word 'dish' in the nursery rhyme line 'And the dish ran away with the spoon'. Reflect on what the dominant culture is in your school and classroom. Identify cultural differences within your class.

Malaguzzi (1920–94) and the Reggio Emilia approach

Key ideas	Impact on the classroom
Reggio Emilia is a town in Italy. The philosophy was created by the community, led by Loris Malaguzzi, in response to the Second World War and a desire to educate children to have freedom of thought after the experiences of the Fascist dictatorship prior to this time. In this approach, children direct their own learning and the role of the adult is to support the children with their interests. The adult is seen as a facilitator rather than a traditional teacher. This philosophy believes children are inherently strong learners, and that the adult needs to support the development of this already inherent trait. This approach has coined the phrase 'the theory of a hundred languages'. This describes the multiple ways children experience the world, learn and express themselves. The Reggio Emilia approach uses a constructivist theory – meaning that children can learn anything if it is presented in the right way. The environment is considered the 'third teacher' alongside other children and adults.	Reflect on your role as a teacher – are you the holder of all knowledge, filling children's empty minds? Or do you see children as already competent learners? Sit beside children and model play rather than telling children what to do. For example, make a playdough model and talk through the steps you are taking. Watch the impact this modelling has on the children. Do they start to copy and modify your ideas? Make the environment work for you. Ensure it is well planned and captures children's interests.

The learning environment

Key takeaways

- A stimulating and well-organised learning environment will support the learning, behaviour and engagement of children.
- Children will become loud, boisterous and run about if they are bored. If this is happening in your classroom, the environment is not supporting children's interests.

The learning environment is central to the early years classroom. A purposeful, well-labelled space that is accessible to all encourages values such as independence and autonomy; respect and order will support the culture you strive to create in your class. Taking care of the environment will take a large amount of your time as a teacher. The time saved in not having to mark books and plan complete lessons (as teachers in other year groups do) will instead be taken up by cleaning, maintaining and designing the learning environment.

As an early years teacher, you will spend a lot of time cleaning. You will be doing things that teachers in other year groups would not consider part of their job. For example, it is likely that the toilet and sink areas will become a part of your life. The role is more physically demanding than in other year groups, such as getting up and down from the floor, shifting bulky equipment such as water trays, and squatting down to be at eye level with the children you are communicating with. There may be elements to the role that are very different from working with older children. For example, you are likely to spend a lot of time in the toilets doing intimate care. This is not often an expectation in other year groups.

The learning environment will offer many learning opportunities. This will be driven by the space and the resources available to you. There is no prescription of what the indoor and outdoor spaces must contain, but there are time-honoured provisions that most early years classrooms aim to provide. If your space is limited, you may consider offering things on a rolling basis and putting things out for limited times. What you want to avoid is having too much out. It is better to provide fewer, high-quality opportunities than to offer a lot of poor ones. This is because clutter will result in disorganisation, and an area covered in broken, disorganised resources will not lead to high-quality play.

While there is no statutory list of resources, using an audit will help you know what you are aiming for. Refer to the extra resources at the end of this book for a simple audit of provision for the indoor and outdoor learning spaces. There are other audits available on the internet or through other providers.

A cluttered classroom that does not offer logical organisation, or high-quality toys and resources, will not lead to high-quality play and learning opportunities. However, high-quality does not mean expensive. High-quality means fit for purpose and attractive to the learners. Resources should be clean and accessible and stored at a height that children can access independently. Open baskets and clear plastic containers make identification of items easier. Labelling each box with the name and an image of the item will support independence, and this will help children to find what they want and to tidy up more quickly.

Zones will help to define learning areas. Try to keep these spaces flexible so they can be expanded or removed throughout the year. To help you feel confident supervising these areas, avoid high barriers. The most effective way of doing this is to use furniture to zone areas. Always ensure furniture is sturdy and can't be tipped or climbed. Be mindful that if you make a clear passageway, children will not be able to avoid the temptation to run through it. Break up large, straight tracks with furniture that will naturally slow down the movement through the space. Mapping out your space will help you think about how the space can best be used to meet the needs of your classroom. Remember to put art areas near sinks, and quieter areas away from noisier ones.

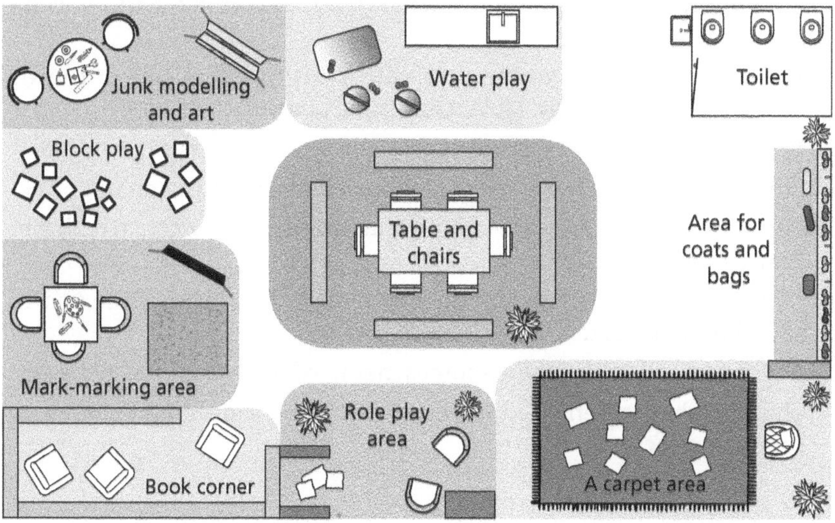

Provide plenty of natural resources for children to touch and play with indoors and out. Children are very attracted to these types of resources. Baskets of pinecones, bark, wood slices, leaves, twigs, stones and seed pods are attractive and can be used in a variety of areas. Be aware of choking or poisoning hazards with natural items and ensure they are not put into mouths. A child with a high level of sensory needs may require extra supervision around these types of resources.

Consider the cohort of children you have in each year group, and adapt the environment to meet their learning, emotional, social and cultural needs. Ensure there are items that reflect the children you have in your class to help them feel a sense of familiarity. The home corner and book area are good places to provide familiar items, books and teddies. Design quiet places for the children to withdraw to. This can be the book area, but ensure it is not placed next to a rowdy activity, such as construction. You should aim to develop a nurturing environment that meets the needs of children throughout the day as they move through full energy levels to feeling tired, quiet or reflective.

The best way to know if a learning environment is meeting the needs of the children is to observe the space during continuous provision time. If you stand back and observe the room, you should see the following:

- Children are spread throughout the space, some in small groups and some individuals.
- All children are focused on what they are doing with a calm atmosphere.
- There is minimal moving around – and no running indoors or flitting from activity to activity. Movement is purposeful.
- There is relative quiet (not raucous).
- Children are posed in a variety of ways – lying, sitting, standing.
- The clusters of children are talking quietly together, co-constructing or sharing discoveries.
- Adults are spread throughout the space, all supporting children and all at children's height.
- Children are accessing the resources they need freely and independently.
- Children that are engaged in their play without needing an adult to keep them focused.

What you don't want to see:

- The whole floor covered in toys and resources.
- Children using items disrespectfully, such as throwing books or standing on toys.
- Adults not engaging with children unless completing an observation.
- Areas with no children in them.
- Running.
- Screaming.
- Children fighting.
- Children clustered around an adult vying for their attention and asking for things.

Involving families

Key takeaway

- Close relationships with families will result in children making greater progress in their learning.

Research, such as that by Siraj-Blatchford et al. (2002) in *Researching Effective Pedagogy in the Early Years*, has demonstrated that schools that have close partnerships with parents have better cognitive outcomes than settings that don't. Most parents are invested in their children's education and the transition to primary school will involve closer relationships between parents and the school than at any other time.

Some ideas of how to develop and promote close relationships with families are given below. These are suggestions only and will need to be chosen sensitively based on the individual context of your setting and the resources available to families outside school.

- **Greet parents at the door.** Ensure you make time for conversation and allow for this in the timetable. Have the support staff inside, dealing with the children, and the teacher standing at the door or gate, offering individual welcomes and creating conversations. Get to know each family well and have daily check-ins. If parents know that information and worries can be easily shared, this will avoid small issues escalating.
- **Send work that children have completed at school to home.** To support two-way information sharing, ask parents to write a Post-it note about the work and then return it to school. This work can be

added to learning journeys or put on display. Work could be a painting, a model, a worksheet or a photo of some learning the child did that day.

- **Have a teddy that can be a home/school link.** A special teddy and their diary can be sent home with children for the weekend. Children and parents can write what they have done with the teddy, and possibly add photos of their adventures. Children love this, and it can be a focus for the child to share with the class, a small group or with a trusted adult at school.
- **Provide weekly updates on learning.** Use a platform such as Teams or Class Dojo and provide weekly updates that relate to the whole class. Include what has been learned that week and reminders about events coming up. This allows busy families to get quick information and to feel they are on top of what is going on at school.
- **Phone home to celebrate achievements.** If a child has done some remarkable learning or made positive steps in development, phone home (or speak face to face at the gate). Make a fuss of the achievements. This will make parents proud, and they will become advocates of you as a teacher, and the work you are doing.
- **Be honest in sharing mistakes or behaviour issues.** If you need to share less-positive news, such as a behaviour issue, show compassion and sum up with praise. It is painful for parents to hear that the most important person in their life is struggling or making poor choices. Parents need to know you always advocate and support their child, even when they are presenting challenging behaviours.
- **Ask questions about the child.** Be interested and take information as true. If parents say a child can count to 20, and they can't do it in school, ask more questions. Find out what is different and be genuinely curious about how learning is supported at home. Avoid implying that learning only happens at school. Trust what parents say and if their experience of a child's learning does not match what you see at school, dig deeper.
- **Have resources at the ready.** If parents need advice or help with something, have some resources to refer them to. This could be as simple as a list of websites to support learning that you can easily refer to and share. Understanding how to help children at home is often bewildering for parents, and ideas of where to look will be gratefully received.
- **Invite parents in.** Ask parents to do a talk or to support the classroom in some way. They have a wealth of expertise. Use parents as volunteers

whenever you can. Parents love to contribute and events like a 'clear up the garden' day bring people together. When parents can help, they feel part of the team, and this brings support and positivity.

- **Do class fundraising events.** This gives parents a feeling of supporting the class. Tell them exactly what the money will be for and make the event easy to arrange. A great example is a 'Big Wheel' event where children are sponsored to bring bikes or scooters to ride around the playground. Parents and family can sponsor the child for each lap they complete.
- **Give specific suggestions about how parents can support learning at home.** For example, rather than saying, 'Read with your child every night', say 'To develop fluency, if a child struggles with a sentence, you say the sentence and then get them to repeat it. This will support fluency.'
- **Do what you say you will.** If you say you are changing reading books on a Friday, then do this. Parents will begin to trust the routine and trust that if you say something will happen, it will. These jobs and dates may seem trivial to a busy teacher, but it supports the development of trust.
- **Ask for help.** Parents love to feel involved. If you need resources for junk modelling, ask parents. If you need support for a trip, ask for volunteers. Always thank parents publicly for their support. A school and a classroom are only as strong as the community surrounding them. If you have willing and helpful parents, thank them and acknowledge the role they play in supporting the school.
- **Hold information evenings** (and ask other staff to help with this). Most parents are very keen to know about how things are taught at school. Some great examples of information evenings are phonics, reading and maths.
- **Home photos on display.** Be sensitive to children's differing circumstances and ask children to bring a picture of 'people who are important to me'. Display these at child height to create a talking opportunity as children show their important people to their friends.
- **Early years section in the newsletter.** Ask if you can have a space in the school newsletter to share learning and celebrate success in the early years. Make what you do every day visible and positive.
- **Activities to try at home.** Have some things that children can borrow from school to do at home. The obvious one is to take a library book home weekly, but you could lend out board games, den-making kits,

treasure baskets, chatterboxes, recipes used at school, song cards and words of songs sung at school.

- **Smile a lot.** If parents feel their child is loved and welcomed, this will do a huge amount towards parents trusting you. This will make coming in to school every day much easier for everyone.
- **Recognise some parents have school anxiety.** School can be difficult for many adults. Drop-off and pick-up times can be difficult for many parents – recognise that not all parents find this an enjoyable experience and be aware that any perceived negative attitude may be hiding anxiety. Starting school is also a reminder that children are growing up quickly, and this can be a difficult transition for many parents. Be gentle with their emotions.

Play

Key takeaways

- Play is the dominant way young children learn.
- There are many types of play.
- Play needs careful planning and preparation.

A dominant ideology still exists in many educational establishments that learning happens when children are sitting at desks, being still and listening to the instructions of an adult. This approach is in stark contrast to the pedagogical approach used when supporting learning through play.

Play may be considered a simplistic activity that children do after learning has taken place; as a recreational activity, rather than the mode of learning. However, play is actually extremely complex and multifaceted.

Play with a specific purpose or learning outcome is difficult to engineer and almost impossible to measure. The same can be said of learning. It is easy to see when play in a classroom is going wrong, but complex to work out how to make it right. In poorly planned environments, play will be noisy, aggressive, sometimes violent, and children will display limited levels of engagement and concentration. High-quality play will see children who are focused and calm, and engaged with high levels of interaction and communication.

Play combines cognitive function with movement, and these are the ingredients needed for all young mammals. Children in early years need to move, therefore they need the space and encouragement to do so. The youngest children in a primary school need the largest space of any year group, and the classrooms need to reflect this. The learning environment should allow movement and be presented on a variety of levels to encourage children to stand, sit, kneel, lie down and move frequently between these types of learning.

The word 'play' is the generic descriptor that describes multiple types of activity. Some examples of different types of play are:

- Heuristic play
- Physical play
- Solitary play
- Onlooker play
- Parallel play
- Associative play
- Cooperative play
- Constructive play
- Expressive play
- Dramatic play
- Competitive play
- Digital play
- Sensory play
- Games with rules.

It is essential that children are immersed in different types of play in different environments. Opportunities for play need to make up at least 50% of the day (Siraj-Blatchford et al., 2002). More detail about this can be found in the section on planning and timetables.

The LEGO® Foundation (Zosh et al., 2017) describes a playful continuum that travels between free play, guided play, games and direct instruction. While all these activities can be a type of play, the support offered by adults varies within these play types, and the level of agency that the child experiences varies from one end of the continuum to the other. All playful learning experiences are important, and each of them is valid in supporting a child's learning and development. The timetable in nursery and Reception should allow for a variety of play types.

Adult directed	Enhanced provision	Continuous provision

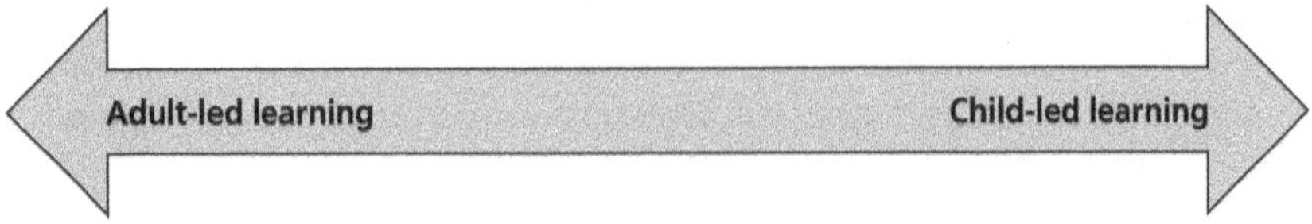

Adult writes a learning objective and the outcome. Child has no control over the direction of the learning.	Adult writes the learning objective but not the outcome. The child has some control over the outcome.	The adult does not write a learning objective or an outcome. The child has control over the direction and outcome of the learning/play.

Learning that is directed by the adult has a pre-defined learning objective and outcome and has been planned in a formal way. The role of the adult is prescriptive and follows a clear sequence. An example would be the teaching of phonics from a scheme. The success criteria or desired outcome is pre-defined and usually links to the long-term curriculum map. This type of learning may be described as adult directed, adult led, adult focused, guided groups, guided play or interventions.

On the other end of the spectrum is free-flow or continuous provision in which learning is directed by the child. Children control the direction of the play, the outcome and how long the play is sustained. The play is fluid and open-ended; it can involve fixed or changeable groups of participants or may be solitary. This type of provision may involve several types of play or one type. It may appear that the adult has no role to play in continuous provision, however, this is where the impact of high-quality interactions occurs. Understanding the role of the adult in supporting play to create a positive interaction is a skilled task, and support staff need to be encouraged and given CPD opportunities to learn about how to scaffold and support play in child-initiated time.

Continuous provision is the time that adults have a role in extending or scaffolding play. Careful scaffolding of the play ensures that the learner is challenged in a cognitive way, and that they can experience the play in a deeper fashion than they could do on their own. The play and the learning are then co-constructed. Siraj-Blatchford et al. (2002) describe this as reflective co-construction. Sylva et al. (2004) use the term 'sustained shared thinking' to describe the process of learning and problem-solving with another. These ideas link to the work of Vygotsky and the Zone of Proximal Development (Vygotsky, 1978) and to Bruner's Joint Involvement episodes (Bruner, 1996). Research such as that conducted in the EPPE study (Sylva et al., 2004) demonstrated that adults co-constructing play with children leads to higher cognitive outcomes.

Co-construction of learning or interactions involves both the adult and the child who must contribute to the thinking and extend it. An adult sitting beside a child and offering questions is not a co-construction. Effective questioning may have a role in scaffolding play, but it can run the risk of interfering with the flow of play. A co-construction could be non-verbal, and the adult and the child work on a project together. While language is vital for development, it is not always a determiner of good adult-to-child co-construction of learning.

Interactions can be initiated by the adult or the child, but the shared element is essential. Children will move towards an adult who is playing and play alongside them. This creates opportunities for play that can be supported and developed by the adult. Adults who do not have specific tasks during continuous provision learning time (such as leading a small group, running an intervention or doing an observation) should be involved in co-construction of play. A warning sign for any early years classroom is seeing adults not involved in co-construction of play during continuous provision play sessions. This indicates the staff team do not understand or value their essential role in interactions and sustained shared thinking. More information about co-construction, interaction and sustained shared thinking can be found in Chapter 3 Research and Perspectives.

Every opportunity to support play should be grasped and every adult working in an early years setting should be aware of this and exploit opportunities as they arise. This is not to say there shouldn't be times when children are left to their own devices and not supported by adults. A skilled practitioner should know (through observation) when to support play and when to let children fully direct the play. This skill needs careful development, and when staff are moved in and out of early years classrooms, without having time to develop skills in interaction, the quality of the learning in that nursery or Reception class will be compromised. This is discussed further in Chapter 4 in the section on managing support staff.

Interactions

Key takeaways

- Co-constructions are a shared interaction between a child and an adult.
- Interactions can be verbal or non-verbal and rely on a trusted relationship.
- The Education Endowment Foundation (EEF) ShREC approach can support interactions.

Interaction is the direct involvement with another. It is a communication that can be verbal or non-verbal and is reciprocal. Strong interactions may use words, body language, facial expressions, gesture and actions. Interactions are most often held between two people who have a warm relationship.

Children should feel safe and trusted in order to overcome the natural power balance between adult and child, and to have the desire to share experiences. A great deal of communication is non-verbal, and children are highly attuned to reading the body language and facial expressions of adults. Being aware of the non-verbal messages you are sending is important. This is even more important when working with children who may have suffered trauma, and who are hypervigilant to reading body language. Positive interactions will only occur when both parties involved in the interaction are relaxed and ready to share ideas.

Positive interactions between adults and children play a crucial role in fostering language development. One sign of a high-quality early childhood environment is when you have to search to locate the adults, as they are all seated at the same level as the children and actively engaged in conversations, seamlessly merging with the surroundings.

Fisher (2016) identified in her book *Interacting or Interfering?* that adults in school have less-natural interactions than occur in a domestic setting. Fisher describes unnatural interactions as those that are not replicated by family and that only educators do. There is an artificial role played by adults who feel the need to question and scaffold learning in a manner that does not reflect children's threads of interest. This has the effect of killing the interaction, as children are wary of forced conversation. Forming natural interactions that extend a child's conceptual development needs practice and conscious thought.

The EEF (2018) identified commonalities in multiple pieces of research of elements that support high-quality interactions. They have abbreviated these areas to the acronym ShREC.

- **Sh** – share attention. Be at the same level as the child and pay attention to what they are engaging with.
- **R** – respond. Follow the child's lead whether it be verbal or non-verbal. Respond to them.
- **E** – expand. Repeat what the child says and add more detail. Model grammatically correct sentences and use strong vocabulary.
- **C** – conversation. Have extended back and forth interactions. Give children time to listen, process and respond.

It is easy to have good verbal interactions with the articulate children in class who are good at conversation and can express themselves well. It is more difficult to have these interactions with children who may have a speech and language delay, a SEND or who have not had the same start in life as their peers and need more support interacting. Spending time with these children is essential to provide the opportunity for them to close some of the communication gaps they have between them and their peers. An appropriate intervention may be as simple as allocating time to play with these children and focus on sustained shared thinking.

Behaviour management

Key takeaways

- Supporting social and emotional skills is central to all aspects of early years teaching.
- Asking children to do things that is beyond their stage of development can lead to challenging behaviour.
- Conflict resolution skills need to be part of the curriculum.
- An insecure attachment may lead to challenging behaviours. This can be supported with a strong key-worker system.

Young children are wonderfully exciting to work with and are full of life and energy. However, the stage of development for this age group means young children are impulsive and often struggle to communicate their wants and needs. Young children are developing their social interaction skills. This means you will need a great deal of patience, and you will need to be realistic about what you expect of young children's behaviour.

You need to embrace the strong emotions young children display as they are a normal part of development. Supporting children to sort through and understand their strong emotions is central to early years education.

Behaviour is a response to a situation or stimulus. Challenging behaviour indicates that a child's needs are not being met. Inversely, positive social behaviour means a child's needs are being met. As an early years teacher, you need to become an expert on reading body language and behaviour as young children are not skilled in using spoken language to express their needs or ideas. If a child is behaving in an antisocial way, you need to consider what need is not being met and make adaptations accordingly. The responsibility for this lies with the adult. Blaming the child is pointless and will not support their development.

Children need to be encouraged to have a voice and be assertive. This can be done by supporting children to talk through their disputes. This supports children to develop their social skills, and to develop thinking towards conflict resolution and concepts that are developmentally challenging for young children, such as sharing. Arguments should not be ignored by adults, and children need to be actively supported through them. Children should not simply be told to stop behaviour without a follow-up conversation as this would be a missed opportunity to help children learn and develop their personal, social and emotional skills.

Resources can be used to support children who struggle with expressive language. An example of this is emotion pictures that children can point to when explaining how they are feeling, or the use of Makaton signs to support oral language. If children are arguing, scratching, biting or throwing things, an adult could spend time with this child, supporting the interaction they want to achieve.

Resources in the classroom to support positive behaviour, such as books, are important for children to be able to access on a regular basis. These can be used in planning, to cover areas of learning that can be referred to during behaviour discussions.

Children should have clear choices and consequences, as they do throughout the school, but consequences should be age appropriate. Consequences for young children should be immediate. Delayed consequences will lose their impact as the child will have mentally moved on from the incident and may not link the consequences to the misdemeanour. The same can be said for rewards. For example, asking a child who has hit another child to go to the headteacher's office and explain what they have done, will add too many variables to the consequence. If the child does not have an existing relationship with the headteacher, and if they are not familiar with the office space, it is likely the child will be focused on the new person and the new space, rather than reflecting on their behaviour or developing skills in order to improve behaviours. They will be so consumed with the new environment that the purpose for the visit is likely to be lost. However, speaking to a known adult in a quiet space about their behaviour is more likely to have an impact. Depending on the situation, a firm 'No' may be enough of a consequence.

Consequences must be simple for young children, but this is even more important when a child has an additional need that may impact processing time or language, such as global development delay, autism, English as an additional language (EAL), or if they are angry. In these situations, excessive use of language is often likely to be misunderstood by the child, who may not be able to understand the words. Young children rely heavily on reading body language, and an awareness of this by the adult is essential. Less language, more overt body language and an appropriate tone of voice is important for a young child to understand the message being relayed. A child will need time to process messages, to calm down and to consider their behaviour. For this reason, you should consider the effectiveness of forcing a child to say sorry to another. You can make this an invitation, but it should not be forced. For example, after a conversation about choices, and after appropriate consequences, you may say, 'Would you like to say sorry?' However, if a child says, 'No' (verbally or non-verbally), this needs to be respected. An apology needs to be genuine, or children learn to follow adult expectations to apologise rather than genuinely feeling remorseful. Children may often choose to show they are sorry in non-verbal ways such as with a hug, or by sharing a toy.

Having high expectations for behaviour is essential, and making allowances for limited vocabulary and verbal expression should not be confused with low expectations. For example, children in a Reception class should be able to sit on their bottoms, with legs crossed and not touching anyone else, for approximately a short, ten-minute input. Of course, there are variables for children with additional needs, but generally, this should be the norm. However, asking the same group of children to do this for 20 minutes may be asking too much. Children of all ages respond very well to praise and other positive reinforcement.

Do this often, and with great flourish, as this body language will support the verbal messages you are giving. Smile a lot and children will want to please you. Positive relationships are the backbone of any behaviour management, regardless of children's age.

Transitions from one activity to another are often a flash point for behaviour issues. This is the same in all year groups, but the attention span and distractibility of young children exemplifies this. For example, if children are asked to come to the carpet, and one child does not, by the time you have spoken to that child and got them to sit down, it is likely that many of the others who did sit down, will now be rolling around the carpet, doing someone's hair or crawling under a desk. Consider the following when transitioning young children from one type of activity to another.

1. Keep the routines the same. As soon as you do something different, you need to expect this to take longer. Build in time for new transitions and activities.
2. Use a non-verbal signal to indicate the transition, such as music or clapping.
3. Follow up every minor distraction or deviation instantly.
4. Have very high expectations and do not deviate from this, even when you are tired.
5. If you give an instruction to sit on the carpet, give a short time for compliance. If you give too long, children will forget what was expected of them and get distracted.
6. Have visual reminders of expectations on display at the carpet area. These should be images of expectations for good sitting such as legs crossed, mouths still, hands in lap.
7. Praise those quickest on the floor and do this in an animated way – this will act as positive reinforcement for the children who aren't complying. Always use very visual praise if possible, such as thumbs up and stickers. What you look for is what you will see. Give more attention to positive behaviours and pay limited attention to the poor behaviours.

Transitions need to be fast and time limited. Children will very quickly pick up when the transition is taking a long time and will find something else to do. Always reflect on whether whole-group sessions can be delivered in a more-effective way, such as in small groups, or during the continuous provision. Whole-class carpet times are very difficult to do well, so if there is a more-effective option, then use it. Do not confuse compliant children with attentive children and don't fall into the trap of thinking it is a requirement to teach whole-class sessions. Always choose the grouping that best suits the learning you are trying to deliver.

Some other hotspots for early years classroom behaviour are detailed below.

Fighting over bikes	• Try a sign-up system and a timer to make the time on a bike fair. This supports maths (time) and writing skills (signing up). • Ensure the strongest and most-dominant children do not monopolise the bikes. Put a system in place to ensure fair access for all.
Not tidying up	• Reduce the number of resources out. • Allocate certain jobs to groups of children. Put adults with the groups that struggle to focus during tidy-up. • Use praise and stickers for those children who are able to tidy up independently. • Put a supporting adult by the children who do not help tidy up.
Not sitting still on the carpet	• Reduce the length of time on the carpet. • Have visual expectations on display and refer to them often. • Praise children who are sitting appropriately. • If a child is not developmentally ready to sit and listen, reduce the expectation, and have the child do small-group or 1:1 work elsewhere. Do not force a child who cannot focus on the carpet to do so. They will not learn, and you will become frustrated.
Pushing in a line	• Let children walk in twos, holding the hand of a partner that they like. • Give praise for the children who can walk nicely. Stickers are very motivational for most young children. • You could hold the hand of a child who is constantly pushing. ➔

Hitting and biting	• Hitting and biting are signs of frustration and are frequently related to social interactions, such as sharing resources. You need to work out what is frustrating the child who is hitting or biting. This child will need support with social interactions and may need some 1:1 support in the areas that cause frustration. For example, if a child loves the trucks and diggers, and struggles to share, they will need support from an adult when other children join this play. You must observe carefully for the times and types of play that may cause these issues and offer support. • If a child is lashing out due to an obsession with a specific toy (i.e. when another child touches it), consider setting this aside for only this child to use. This is not always possible, but setting aside one car or one doll may save everyone a lot of stress. You need to choose your battles.
Running around inside	• Place furniture so there are no natural corridors to build up speed. • Give constant verbal reminders that running is for outside.
Shouting out at carpet times	• An impulsive child may need support from an adult beside them, so they can share their ideas quietly without disrupting anyone else. This child may be better suited to a smaller, key-group approach rather than to carpet times. • Give verbal reminders not to shout out. • Use visual reminders about carpet-time expectations.

The advice described above is successful when used with most children. It is likely, however, that there will be children in your class who require an additional or adapted approach, whether they are SEND related or due to adverse early experiences. In these cases, it is important that you get additional support from other professionals, such as the special educational needs coordinator (SENCO), to ensure that both the child and you are receiving appropriate support.

It is likely that at least one child in your class will demonstrate behaviour related to attachment issues. Attachment is a term used in psychology to refer to the relationship between a child and their parent, or primary caregiver. The quality and stability of this relationship is described as having a permanent impact on areas of development such as sense of self, self-esteem and development of relationships with others.

There are several types of attachment, such as secure attachment, ambivalent attachment, avoidant attachment and disorganised attachment. The style that best serves a content, well-adjusted child is a secure attachment. Describing the other types is beyond the scope of this book, but they can easily be researched on the internet. Knowing a little about attachment can help to describe some of the difficulties children may face in their lives and may help describe some behaviours you see in young children. It explains why it is important for young children to have an adult at school who is a familiar, trustworthy key worker that they see every day. Children often choose their own trusted adult. If you are using key workers, it may be best to set these groups a few weeks into term rather than at the start so you can get a feel for which children are best placed with which adults.

Early trauma will have a marked impact on behaviour. You may be aware of this trauma if a child is in local authority care, under a child protection order or adopted, but you are likely to have other children who have suffered trauma which is unknown to services or to the school. Training on Adverse Childhood Experiences (ACES) will help you understand the impact of trauma on a child, and this will help you understand behaviour more. Ask your headteacher or SENCO how you can access this training.

Schemas are well understood in the early years, but less well known by Primary teachers. Schemas are most observable in younger children, and by the time they attend Primary school, many schemas have been resolved. However, it is possible that many children in the first year of school may display schematic play, and so understanding schemas will help to identify and support such children.

A schema is a strong drive to repeat behaviours that supports learners to discover how things function. It supports brain development and can be described as a fascination. Repeating and practising actions supports learning. It helps children make connections between actions in varied environments and situations, and apply knowledge/patterns to different situations.

Schematic play can involve the following:

Trajectory schema	throwing objects, climbing, jumping, running-water fascination, drawing straight lines
Transporting schema	carrying things and moving resources from one place to another →

Rotational schema	turning things, winding things, spinning hoops, rolling tyres, spinning
Enclosing schema	wrapping things up, putting paper in envelopes, hiding in tents, laying in tunnels, staying in dens, getting in boxes
Enveloping schema	covering up items with other resources, wrapping up toys with blankets and paper, folding notes to put in pockets
Connecting schema	joining things together or putting them end-to-end in a line, connecting pipes and gutters, connecting trains

If you observe schematic play, you should plan experiences to allow the child to explore the schema. Some children may fixate on schemas, but most children will move beyond this type of play when they have been supported to explore and develop their thinking.

Outdoor learning and risky play

Key takeaways

- Outdoors is a unique learning environment and should not replicate the indoor environment.
- Children need to play outdoors every day for a large percentage of the day.
- Keeping your outdoor area clean and fresh will take considerable effort. Timetable this in daily and involve all adults to lighten the load.

Most children will display high levels of involvement and engagement when learning outdoors. This space needs to provide more than just a large area for children to run around and let off steam, and the outdoor provision needs planning in line with indoor planning. Staff working in an early years classroom need to understand that they will be outside for extended periods, in all weathers. Staff will need to come to work in clothing appropriate for all weathers and members of the SLT need to understand that staff in early years classrooms will need to have a more relaxed attire in order to work appropriately. If adults are cold or uncomfortable outdoors, they will not want to go outside, so it is important that the routine allows for staff to rotate between indoors and outdoors, and that there is extra care to support each other's comfort and wellbeing.

Outdoor learning will provide a different learning experience to indoors. Many children who struggle to concentrate or settle indoors will present differently outdoors. The weather, space and freedom of the outdoors appeals to children in a way the indoors may not. Outdoor learning opportunities can offer children time and space to explore and discover insects, plants, stones and mud. Children can be loud, excited and physical in their discoveries and move freely from one space to the other, with great fluidity. Children can be more hands-on with each other and there are more opportunities to flex large muscle groups as items are hauled about. The outdoors has a positive impact on wellbeing and children can experiment with things, such as constructing large structures and working collaboratively to complete a task.

Outdoors offers more opportunities for risky play, where children can develop resilience, use problem-solving skills and test their own boundaries. They can develop skills, such as spatial awareness, and have more sensory opportunities as they are immersed in the weather and hear environmental sounds, such as birdsong.

The outdoor provision needs careful planning, and you need to factor into the week additional time to maintain it to a high standard. This space needs frequent sweeping, replenishing and washing down. The nature of the play will mean the outdoor space will get very messy, and children will spread resources further than indoors. For example, sandpits will support sustained collaborative play for many children, but areas around the sand need to be easy to sweep and sand needs to be replenished frequently.

Outdoor spaces can be expensive to maintain and this needs to be budgeted for. Planting areas are attractive and add great value, encouraging wildlife and insects, but require a keen gardener on the staff team to keep on top of weeding and replanting. The outdoors is easiest to manage when the whole staff team contribute. Having timetabled time to work on the outdoors together will lighten the burden. For example, having all staff out from 8.30–8.40 and again from 3.15–3.30 every day will help to manage this space.

Risky play

Risky play is described as play where inherent risks are involved in the task. Risky play from a young age supports children to learn their own limitations and the boundaries of their bodies and the world around them. Some examples of risky play are given at the top of the next page.

- Jumping off tree stumps onto the ground.
- Using a climbing frame.
- Walking along a plank.
- Walking in the wilderness (with the dangers of stinging nettles, tree roots as tripping hazards, etc.).
- Climbing trees.
- Using the saws on the tinker table.
- Play fighting.
- Riding bikes.

It is essential that children participate in risky play as the benefits can outweigh the risks, assuming the play is conducted in a safe and planned manner. The adults running the activities should be comfortable with the level of risk and do a risk assessment in order to minimise the chance that children will be hurt or scared during an activity.

Parents need to be well informed of the purpose of risky play so they understand the benefits of this type of activity. They need details of how activities are managed and what support children will be offered. Anxious parents need to know that their child will be expected to take risks, and understand that this is a normal part of development for young children.

The advantages of risky play include:

- Fun and exhilaration.
- A sense of achievement and confidence building.
- Developing an awareness of risk and how to manage it.
- Improvement in fitness, flexibility and coordination.
- Developing problem-solving skills.
- Developing teamwork skills.
- Developing independence.
- Learning about your own limits.
- Learning how the world works, such as the basic laws of physics (e.g. gravity) and the laws of engineering (e.g. a wide base makes a structure stronger).

When planning risky play consider the following:

1. Ensure you have risk assessed the play and minimised the risks as far as possible. Remember there is a difference between risky play and dangerous play. Make sure there is nothing dangerous on offer. A risk assessment does not always need to be written down. A discussion with staff about the activity, and support needed for children to access it, is a risk assessment. For example, children stacking crates to climb should not be allowed to build higher than waist level. Check with the SLT about the expectations for written risk assessments at your school.
2. Ensure children are specifically taught the skill/task in a controlled way. Clear modelling by the adult is essential. For example, when learning to use the saw on the tinker table, you should teach the parts of the saw, explain how the blade cuts, explain how to safely hold the saw, demonstrate safety (such as using a clamp to hold the wood and wearing eye goggles), show how both hands need to be on the saw and then model how to cut. You can then use backward fading (Sherrington and Caviglioli, 2020) to ensure children understand the steps, before they can have a turn closely observed by the adult. Over time, the children can be trusted to use the saw independently.
3. Allow time and space for this type of play and ensure you provide adequate supervision when it is a new skill. Trust children to know what they can and can't do and support them with this.
4. Be aware of your perceptions towards risky play and gender. Ensure boys and girls get equal access to this sort of play. Be mindful about language used when boys and girls choose this type of play, as unconscious bias is easily passed on to children.

For more reading on risky play, look up the following excellent, free book by Tim Gill: *No Fear. Growing up in a risk adverse society* by Tim Gill (2007). Free online at: https://timrgill.files.wordpress.com/2010/10/no-fear-19-12-07.pdf

Assessment and observation

Key takeaways

- Observation is the main form of assessment in early years.
- There are many types of observations, each with a different focus.
- You must timetable in observations and reflections frequently.

Most of the assessment done in Primary school is through formal assessment, whether this be standardised or not. More recently there has been a move towards checking for understanding and supporting memory through quizzes as a formative assessment. These methodologies don't work in early years, as children are unable to write test papers, and you may end up testing the wrong thing, such as whether a child can write coherently rather than whether they have retained and understood the knowledge you are trying to test.

Assessment in the form of small tasks can help to determine whether a child has understood a concept. For example, asking a child to count out eight objects will help you see whether they can demonstrate 1:1 correspondence and can count in order. Assessments like this can be useful and form a picture of knowledge of some areas of the curriculum. However, other parts of the curriculum such as language, socialisation and application of knowledge are best assessed through observation.

Observation and the development of planning – that reflects the next steps identified in the observation – are interlinked. Responsive planning is how teachers ensure that the learning environment, and the directed teaching, are quickly meeting the rapidly evolving needs of the learners.

Observations may be formal or informal and it is essential that time is allowed for this. The cycle between observation and planning is as follows.

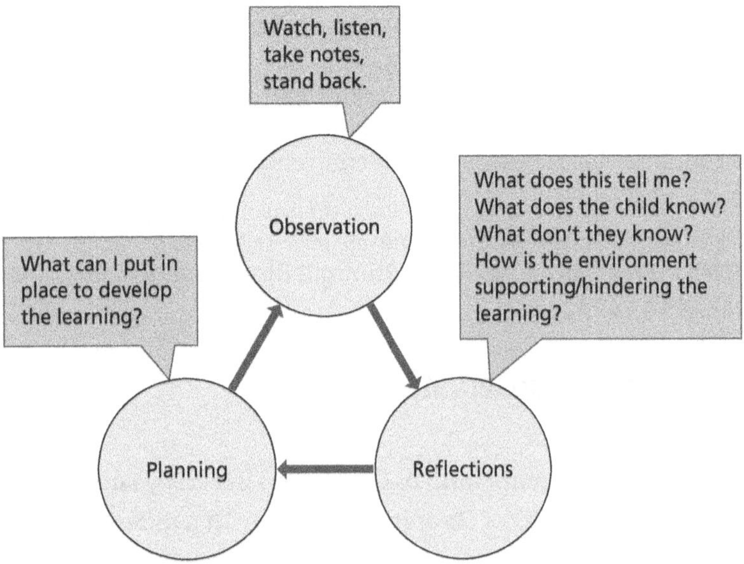

Standing back and watching the classroom and children is a necessary part of the daily routine, as this is how you will measure the impact of the environment, identify the progress of individuals and reflect on the social interactions of individuals and groups. Observations need to be done both on the spot, as you see them, and scheduled as part of the timetable. Making time for observations needs to be a priority if you want to plan lessons and activities that will closely reflect children's stage of learning. If you are spending every part of the day completing tasks such as teaching groups, setting up the environment or leading whole-class sessions, and do not timetable observations, then you will miss opportunities to see the learning and interactions happening in play.

Teachers and support staff have told me they feel nervous about taking time to stand back and observe the provision in case it appears like they are doing nothing. Out of guilt, or worry as to how this will look, staff may fill time with tasks such as cleaning up and tidying. You need to be confident to prioritise observations and guard time to do this effectively.

There are many types of observations that you can do. Some examples are:

- narrative observations (long observation)
- snapshot observations – notes or photos
- group observations
- the Leuven Scale (wellbeing and involvement)
- observations of use of the environment (where in the environment the children are choosing to play)
- time sample intervals (what a child does at different time intervals).
- tracking
- quality of interactions – observation between adult to child and child to child
- learning stories
- sociogram
- work samples (such as a learning journey).

Each of these types of observation has a different purpose, and you need to consider what you are trying to find out before you choose the type of observation.

To support spontaneous observations, you need to have the tools for observation ready and easy to access. Some things you can do to ensure you are always ready for an observation are listed on the following page.

- Wear an apron with Post-it notes or observation sheets in large pockets.
- Put Post-it notes or observation forms around the environment.
- Use technology and software to take photos and quickly link to individual profiles.
- Timetable observation time and ensure all staff are involved in this. Take turns completing observations at different points in the timetable.

Refer to the extra resources at the end of this book for some examples of observation proformas you may choose to adapt and use.

Planning and timetables

Key takeaways

- You will need to have long-term, medium-term and short-term plans. The short-term plans will include adult-directed, enhanced and continuous-provision plans.
- Assessment (observation) and planning need to be amalgamated as one process.

Planning the curriculum and considering the sequence of lessons is vital to focused and ambitious learning in all year groups, but planning in early years is different from that done in the rest of the Primary school. In early years, you will need to let go of the concept of planning in advance. While some elements of early years curriculum can be planned ahead of time, much of it will need to be short term, flexible, reactive and planned in the moment. It is highly likely that sessions you plan will change and be modified, and timescales for activities will change rapidly due to children's engagement and interest levels. Trusting children to lead learning is exciting but it requires letting go of control. This can be quite a challenge when your training and experience have pushed the model of the teacher standing at the front of the class, instructing children, who sit passively at desks.

The purpose of planning is so that the teacher can prepare learning that is ambitious and well resourced. Planning documents are fluid and regularly adapted. There is no one form of planning, as there are variables such as size of the school, the unit to be taught and the experience of the teacher. If you don't know where to start, you can access planning exemplars (refer to the extra resources at the end of this book), but use these with caution. They are only one example of how planning may be presented. They are a model to be adapted, or totally ignored, at your own discretion.

Long-term planning

This planning consists of the curriculum documents that demonstrate the learning intent for the year. This will be agreed by the SLT and governors and is unlikely to change each year. Schools may call this the curriculum map for the year group and it should reflect the government curriculum such as the early years foundation stage (EYFS) in England. This planning, although unique to the EYFS, needs to be developed in such a way that it is a coherent journey through EYFS with clear connection to the national curriculum (NC) from Year 1 onwards. This is not a moving of NC content into EYFS, but rather a development of an awareness of what will be learned in EYFS that will go on to support later learning in Year 1 and above. Subject leads in the school need to be aware of what is happening in early years and know how this knowledge is built on in later year groups. EYFS planning should not, therefore, be subject-specific as in later years, but there should be an awareness of what children's learning will likely be in EYFS that will later become individual subjects. This document will demonstrate how early years are not separate to the other year groups but are the foundation for later learning.

This planning is likely to be presented on one or two pages of A4, as a grid. It will cover all terms in the year and have a short description of coverage for each area. This planning may be available to parents and stakeholders on the school website.

Medium-term planning

Medium-term planning will offer more detail than the long-term planning. It is likely that this planning already exists and needs little modification. This is very similar to medium-term planning in other year groups and lays out the intentions for different topics throughout each term. These may be supported by knowledge organisers (for teachers) and are broad in their intentions. Medium-term planning should not include specific information, such as resources and activities. Instead, it should include the topics and general learning objectives. Medium-term plans may be thematic, but these themes should be loose.

Knowledge organisers may be used to share the learning for the term with families and adults. They are a broad-brush approach to what will be covered throughout the term and provide a summary of the loose themes and key knowledge to be covered in a unit, including vocabulary and key learning. A knowledge organiser could make links to other subject areas. These are concise documents (no more than two pages of A4) and contain pictures and grids for easy reference.

Weekly/short-term planning

There are several types of provision you need to cover in your short-term planning. These are on a continuum from precise objectives and outcomes to no objectives or outcomes.

Adult-directed session	Enhanced provision	Continuous-provision session

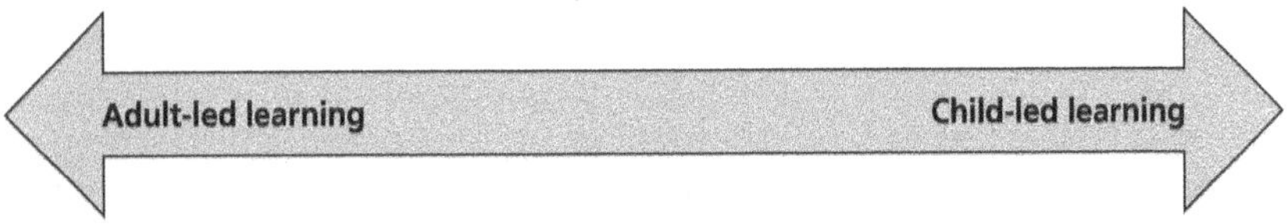

Adult writes a learning objective and the outcome. Child has no control over the direction of the learning.	Adult writes the learning objective but not the outcome. The child has some control over the outcome.	The adult does not write a learning objective or an outcome. The child has control of the direction and outcome of the learning/play.

Adult-directed sessions are those that can only be taught directly by an adult. An example of this is phonics, handwriting or some mathematical concepts, such as number bonds. These sessions will be 10–20 minutes in length and will be very prescriptive. However, they do not have to be taught to a whole class but could be delivered to a small group or 1:1. An intervention is an example of an adult-directed session.

If you are using a scheme, this planning may be provided for you, so your time needs to be spent becoming familiar with the sequence, and amending the plan to your style and the needs of the class. Spend time adapting these plans rather than thinking you can teach straight from the plan, as this will be too generic to meet the needs of your class.

If you are not using a scheme, you will need to consider the learning objective of the lesson, the resources, the activities and the desired outcomes. These sessions often act as an introduction to other areas of the provision. For example, you may read a book to the children, introducing specific vocabulary. You then anticipate they will use this vocabulary later in their play or it will be used with enhancements. You may also use adult-focused sessions to model a sequence of activities that will then be part of the continuous provision or as an enhancement.

As an example, if the learning objective is to paint a picture in the style of Monet, you may do the following as a sequence of adult-focused lessons prior to asking children to do a painting in the art area.

1. Introduce Monet as an artist and learn about his life.
2. Look at some of his art on the whiteboard and consider the materials he used and the subject matter of his art.
3. Model painting the *Water Lilies and Japanese Bridge* painting, copying the real image.
4. Instruct the children that they need to do a painting of their own at some time during the week on the art table. Explain this is the only art they will be doing this week. Place your painting and any example Monet images on the table as a model. This task then moves from an adult-focused task to enhanced provision.

Enhanced provision is when you have written a specific learning objective, and resources are suggested to support the development and scaffolding of that learning. However, the outcome of the session is controlled by the children. In the example detailed above, the children will paint a picture of water lilies, but they control how long they spend on their work, whether they do more than one painting, and what the finished product looks like. Adults may support this process, or they may not.

Another example of this is making a tuff tray with a scenery and small-world characters from a story you have been reading. The objective could be for children to retell the story. Children may end up taking this play in a different direction, but the learning objective for that area should be considered in the planning by the adults.

Continuous provision is provision that does not have specific learning objectives but has broad, sweeping objectives that will have been identified in the long- and medium-term planning. The planning for continuous provision will involve considerations for what you need to gather to support the environment. Things put out for continuous-provision planning may reflect observations done on children the week before, of their interests and learning fascinations. Most of the resources within the continuous provision will not change, allowing children to become familiar with what they may find in this area. Examples of this are the blocks in the block area, or the kitchen in the home corner. Observing how the children are playing in the continuous provision will allow you to plan in the moment, and develop high-quality interactions.

The process of planning

These are the suggested steps to follow when writing your weekly planning:

1. Have medium-term plans and any schemes, such as phonics, on hand. Identify what part of the sequence of lessons you are up to, and where these need to be taught. Block them in on a timetable. You could mark off objectives from a medium-term plan as you teach them to ensure you cover everything you need to over the term.
2. Consider the observations that you have done this week. What areas of interest or areas to develop can be put into the planning this week? Make a brief list of these areas.
3. Consider which aspects of point 1 and 2 can be taught in the continuous-provision sessions, and which aspects need to be taught as adult-directed sessions. Plot each of these in place either on the continuous-provision plan, or on the lengthier weekly planning sheets.
4. Write detailed adult-directed plans that have not been provided by a scheme.
5. Fill any gaps in the continuous-provision plan with general activities. These do not need a learning objective, as you will need to observe the children's interests and engagements with this area over the week. It is okay to have gaps. Do not complete every box unnecessarily.
6. Put up plans for all staff to see. Remember, these will be amended as the week progresses. Write on them, cross out things that no longer apply and carry items forward. Be fluid with your planning.

Timetable

Your timetable needs to be flexible but should offer a familiar routine so children can feel secure in knowing what is coming next and can develop an understanding about the flow of the day. You will struggle to teach more than three discrete English and maths lessons a week. Think about what areas of the curriculum can be put into the continuous provision, to reduce these sessions down. You will need to teach phonics five days a week.

If Reception children currently attend whole-school assemblies, consider dropping some or all of these until the end of the summer term. Attending smaller-phase assemblies may be more suitable for this age group.

Consider delivering snacks through a café-style provision to reduce the amount of carpet time children have. This involves setting aside a table and having the fruit, milk and water out for children to access when they are ready. The advantages of this are that children learn independence and can decide when they eat, so it does not interrupt the flow of their deeper play. If you are worried that children are not having a drink or snack, you can use a system like self-registration to monitor who has attended the table. For example, if children have a snack, they put a lolly stick with their name on it in the tin. Ten minutes before the snack table is tidied up, children who have not attended the snack table can be called over. Give children jobs as helpers to cut fruit and set up and tidy away the snack café. Spray bottles with water, and cloths and aprons make this sort of job very appealing and children relish the opportunity to help with adult jobs. This will support their developing independence.

Lunchtimes will likely be decided by the whole-school routine. All adults need their allotted lunch break, and the dining-hall timings will be tightly scheduled. For most schools, Reception children will need to join the main playground for the lunch break. Once the initial transition routines of support have been delivered, children will manage this well, and will enjoy spending time with older children in a different play space to their own classroom and garden. Some settings ensure that EYFS children wear a hi-viz vest during the lunchtime play with older children for the first term so that they are easily identified and they can be monitored to ensure they are safe and happy.

Refer to the extra resources at the end of this book for a sample timetable.

Writing

Key takeaways

- Children need good fine motor control of their hands and fingers to be able to write.
- Handwriting should be taught 1:1 or in small groups.
- Modelling writing every day is essential as it gives children an awareness of the application of writing in real life.

Physical development

To write with accuracy, children need to have hand coordination, grasp strength, pincer grasp, hand-to-eye coordination and precision. To learn all this, children must have good fine motor skills and coordination to be able to form letters.

As well as fine motor skills, children need: good core strength; shoulder, arm, elbow, wrist and hand control; an ability to coordinate both sides of their body; and an ability to cross the midline. These gross motor skills are developed not necessarily through writing itself but through play, including climbing, swinging, balancing, rolling, carrying (e.g. buckets of sand and water), digging, stacking and dragging large objects (e.g. crates and logs), and dancing. These gross motor skills need to be proactively provided for and developed in order for children to be successful writers. Rushing to formal writing and attempting to leapfrog these physical-development elements should be avoided. Children need adequate time and opportunity to build these essential physical skills.

Fine-motor-skill activities should always be available, and the activity needs to be changed regularly to increase challenge and to keep interest levels high. Children who struggle with fine motor control are less likely to use these areas out of choice. Fine motor activities can be done as an intervention for children who need extra support on these activities, or this can be an adult focus during continuous provision sessions. Difficulties with fine motor control that are not addressed will persist throughout a child's schooling. Difficulties with pencil grip are more difficult to correct the more ingrained motor patterns become.

Some examples of fine motor activities that will support hand strength and coordination are:

- threading beads on shoelaces
- using paintbrushes in shaving foam on a tuff tray
- crafts and cutting with scissors
- peg boards
- spooning fine items into small containers, e.g. rice into small jars
- picking items up with tweezers and tongs
- sewing lace cards
- pick-up sticks
- sorting items into ice-cube trays
- dough
- colouring, tracing and stencil activities
- putting pegs on the side of a container or line
- using paperclips and bulldog clips on paper
- painting with water or paint using thin brushes.

Seating position and posture

In order to assume the correct posture for writing, children will need significant core strength as they will need to support their body, neck and head while they are writing. This is why it is essential to develop this strength through play and physical activity. Be aware of children who may seem to lean on the table or use their elbows to support their bodies or who appear to assume a floppy position, as this may indicate a lack of core strength. For writing, the 90-90-90 position is often encouraged. This means that feet are flat on the floor, and ankles, knees and elbows each form a 90-degree angle. Often, furniture in settings does not allow for a correct writing position, so in areas where there are chairs and tables for practising writing, these need to be at the correct height. Children will write across the classroom and in all areas of provision using a range of postures such as lying or kneeling, but when sitting at tables specifically to write, such as in a 1:1 or small-group input, the 90-90-90 posture should be encouraged.

Vocabulary

Children will enter your classroom with a vast spectrum of vocabulary development. If children have a vocabulary gap between them and their peers, this gap will increase year on year, impacting learning, if these children do not receive additional support. The size of a child's vocabulary in early years is a significant predictor of academic success in all education phases.

Comprehension is dependent on a strong vocabulary. Being able to decode a word does not help a child understand its meaning. The exploration of words and their meanings should happen continuously in the classroom and the quality of interactions between a child and the adult should always be a priority.

Vocabulary will be developed in formal ways, such as through books and in topic work, but also in the conversations that happen constantly throughout the day. Adults should always model sentences with ambitious vocabulary and encourage children to experiment with using more-ambitious words. Each week, new vocabulary needs to be introduced, and all adults need to try and thread these words into their conversations with children. The EYFS setting should be alive with purposeful chatter, and rich with talk and exploring language both between peers and between adults and children.

Mark making and writing with a purpose

All parts of the provision need to support writing. There should be opportunities to write throughout the indoor and outdoor environment. Children should be given the opportunity to support all their learning with writing and should not have to look far for writing implements. There is nothing more frustrating than having an idea that you want to write, and then not being able to find paper or pencil to do so.

Some ideas of resources to place indoors and outdoors to support writing are:

- clipboards and paper
- storage caddies with handles that can be moved around containing pencils, paper and Post-it notes
- labels for models – children must label their model if they want to put it up for display
- a shared writing line, where children can peg up writing they have done for others to see
- large paper and pens on the carpet
- a box of chalk outside
- painting equipment with a variety of brush types – very thin to thick
- whiteboards and pens
- writing on a touch screen
- drawing with sticks, leaves and natural materials in sand/mud
- post-it notes
- large mounted whiteboards in construction or creative areas
- rolls of wallpaper or rolled paper hung from the wall and accessed via a small stepladder to encourage large movements
- perspex sheets and whiteboard pens
- safety mirrors to draw around reflections
- tracing activities including shadow tracing and coloured-light tracing.

Refer to the extra resources at the end of this book for more ideas on how to include resources for writing throughout the environment.

Handwriting

Correct letter formation is not something that can be taught through play. This is an area of learning that is best taught directly by an adult.

Incorrect motor patterns are very difficult to correct and corrections need to be given immediately as the child is writing. Due to the need for immediate correction, handwriting needs to be taught 1:1 or in small groups as it is impossible to monitor a whole class as they form letters.

There is no need to spend time teaching joined writing in early years. Children need to master the correct directionality of letters. If they can do this, then they can learn to join writing in future years. Handwriting sessions can be short and should be done frequently. Ideally, when children are showing they are ready to form letters formally, they could have five minutes a day practising specific letters. Many phonics schemes include this within the sessions. Be aware that children will not show all this readiness at the same time. If children are reluctant to write, spend more time on fine motor activities.

Correct letter formation follows from lots of experience drawing patterns, shapes and a variety of lines. Play and opportunities for mark making in provision need to be rich and varied in order to support readiness for formal letter formation.

Maths

Key takeaways

- Young children cannot understand abstract concepts without opportunity to root this thinking in concrete experience. To support this, they need to use manipulatives to develop mathematical thinking.
- Adults should model graphical mathematics frequently.

Piaget's theory of cognitive development applies to all types of learning but is very evident when teaching mathematics. Children who are asked to work in abstract ways before they are ready will struggle to understand the concepts being taught or will have a shallow and inflexible understanding of the content. This means that they are unable to apply what they know to other situations which they will be required to do. This is often evident when children appear to 'know how to count' as they have just learned one of the early stages of number, which is knowing the number names in order. This does not mean they understand the cardinal and ordinal properties of each number – their order and their worth – they have simply learned the names. The preoperational stage of cognitive development is generally considered to be between 2 and 7 years of age. Prior to this, children are in the sensorimotor stage, which is dominated by learning through the senses and through actions.

The preoperational stage sees children begin to use language and mental images more, and they begin to understand categorisation and can identify similarities and differences when categorising. Within this phase, children are developing the ability to use mental representations rather than rely on the physical appearance of objects or people. This means children can understand that counters can represent sweets when problem-solving or understand a tally may represent the number of laps completed on the bike. Within this stage, children have not developed reversibility. This means thinking is very concrete and children cannot use logic and they cannot transform, combine or separate ideas. Children in this stage will struggle with conservation, which is understanding that the quantity of a group of items remains the same whether they are spread out or in a close group together. Young children can only focus in one dimension at a time.

In order to support children to progress through the preoperational stage, they need to be immersed in activities that will support the development of several areas of learning. Any maths curriculum for early years needs to include each of these areas of learning and their associated concepts.

Learning	Concepts to cover
Cardinality and counting	**One-to-one principle:** to be able to assign one number name to each object that is being counted, including in an irregular positioning. **Stable-order principle:** understanding that when counting, the numbers must be said in a certain order. Children need to be able to count forward and cross the 10s boundaries. **Cardinal principle:** understanding that the number name assigned to the final object in a group is the total number of objects in that group. **Abstraction principle:** understanding you can count things that cannot be touched, such as beats in music. **Conservation:** understanding that the order in which we count a group of objects does not change the quantity and that reorganised groups retain the same quantity if nothing is taken away. **Subitising:** recognising small quantities without the need to count. **Numeral denotation:** to be able to match the written numeral symbol to a quantity. →

Learning	Concepts to cover
Comparison	Understanding some numbers are worth more or less than others. To know that when counting forward, the next number is always worth more. To understand the idea of 'more than', 'less than' and 'equal to' in regard to group sizes. To know that the size of an object in a group does not mean more (smaller items can have the same quantity as larger items).
Composition	To know a whole can be made up of parts in groups of items and in numbers. To know inverse operations of adding and subtracting.
Pattern	Seeking relationships in patterns. To be able to copy and continue a simple repeated pattern and to identify errors in patterns. To be able to make their own pattern.
Shape and space	Developing visual skills and spatial awareness, including positional language. To develop an understanding of the properties of 2D and 3D shapes. To play with translation, rotation and reflection. To identify similarities between shapes and items in the environment.
Measures	Comparing attributes. Using equal units. Positional concepts. Estimating and predicting. Beginning to understand a concept of time.

Throughout each of these principles, children need to be developing mathematical vocabulary and playing with mathematical graphics.

Mathematical activities need to be available to children throughout the day and in multiple areas of the environment. Children do not learn maths as a discrete subject and you need to capitalise on children's mathematical interests in as many areas of play as possible. For example, adding tape measures to the tinker table will encourage children to consider length in their constructions.

You will be expected to teach maths as adult-directed lessons, and it is likely you will need to use a published scheme of work in line with the rest of the school. While these are usually high-quality, be mindful about how long children are expected to concentrate for in directed sessions. Use small-group sessions where possible as children can form misconceptions in mathematics easily, and so concepts are better acquired with higher levels of support. Key groups rather than whole groups will support this.

Refer to the extra resources at the end of this book to see a suggested list of mathematical resources for the learning environment.

Rhymes and songs are a great way to support number development. Children should sing every day, and counting songs can be sung quickly, between sessions, as a time filler. Likewise, books featuring mathematical concepts should be part of the class library.

Resources to support mathematical graphics and mark making need to be readily available to children to help them organise their thoughts and communicate these with others. Children can be encouraged to record mathematical thinking using tallies, numbers, diagrams, directions, graphs and grids. Adults should model writing mathematical thinking in formal and informal ways and children should initially be encouraged to develop their own system for recording their ideas and thinking.

Reading and phonics

Key takeaways

- Phonics teaching should be supported by instilling the love of books and reading for pleasure.
- Stories, rhymes and songs should be part of the daily provision.
- Books should feature in all aspects of the environment, and not only in the book corner.

Most schools in England use a DfE-approved phonics scheme for delivering their phonics curriculum. These schemes have a tightly prescribed sequence that must be delivered as specified. Some schemes are more rigorous than others, with some variance in expectations regarding whether children should sit at chairs, whether it is taught whole class or in groups, and the type of resources that can be used to support the sessions.

The need to provide fidelity within these schemes may cause friction with the pedagogical approach used in early years classrooms. However, the decision on how to deliver phonics is likely to be made by the SLT and so teachers will need to adhere to this curriculum as it will represent a whole-school approach. If you have not had CPD in the delivery of the phonics scheme your school is using, you need to speak to your SLT about getting this as soon as possible to ensure you understand all elements of the approach, as each scheme differs in delivery and materials.

If you do have a say in deciding what scheme the school will adopt:

- Avoid a scheme that expects children to sit at a desk for longer than 20 minutes. An expectation to sit for a long period does not correlate with young children's physical development or attention spans.
- Choose a scheme with a variety of books that children can access. All scheme books will be decodable, but having freedom to buy a variety of books will support a diversity of genres and offer a varied reading diet.
- Find a scheme that is only delivered once a day. More than this will eat into your continuous provision time, which will limit your ability to provide a broad, balanced curriculum.
- Look for one that is easily adaptable for a variety of abilities.
- Look for one that offers intervention support for children who need additional support.
- Ensure the scheme does not come with a costly CPD price. This often dramatically increases the cost of the scheme over time. This CPD is more than a one-off cost as staff coming new to the school will need this training. This on-going cost can be overlooked when comparing scheme prices.
- Ensure that the scheme does not require costly annual licences or subscriptions (i.e. for the same reason as in the previous point).

Multiple research studies demonstrate that phonics is the most effective method of teaching reading for most children (EEF, 2021). While high-quality phonics teaching is vital, teachers must not forget that learning to read should be supported by engagement with books and print in a variety of genres. Every child should be borrowing library books, listening to an adult read, sharing books with other children, identifying sight words, being immersed in print around the room, seeing the real-life applications of print, hearing a variety of genres, and singing songs and rhymes.

The reading provision should extend beyond phonics, and the classroom should embed a culture where books, vocabulary and reading are high on the agenda. Children need to hear books and rhymes every day. The stories you select to read to the children need to be high quality and should offer a variety of text types. You should consider issues such as disability, equality and gender to ensure that stereotypes are avoided and to allow story times to become a prompt for further discussion and work.

Do not assume that any books or rhymes are known by all the children. Some children may have had limited exposure to books or songs, or they may have experienced stories and songs culturally different to your own.

Books shared with children should be left out on display in the environment for children to access in their own time. You should revisit favourite stories several times to develop vocabulary and deepen understanding of the storyline. Books can be placed as part of enhancements to encourage children to retell the story with props and to access stories in a different context to how they were initially introduced.

Books should be everywhere in EYFS, both inside and outside. There is a temptation to keep books only indoors but this can send a message about where and when books should be enjoyed and explored. Having an outside reading shed, den or reading trolley with quieter and more-comfortable outdoor spaces can encourage children to read in the fresh air and to enjoy reading across all of the provision. This goes for storytime or read-aloud sessions too. These are often only ever held indoors but creating a space in outdoor provision or visiting another area of the school grounds can provide beautiful and alternative settings in which to share books.

Modelling

Key takeaway

- Modelling is vital in early years and can be done in a variety of ways.

Modelling is an essential pedagogical approach when teaching in the early years. Young children struggle to visualise abstract concepts; they have a very short attention span and have limited life experiences onto which to hang new ideas. For these reasons, the adult should provide worked examples accompanied with a clear explanation and demonstration of each step.

Modelling needs to be broken down into much smaller chunks than for older children. Each step needs to be clear and unambiguous. Most modelling can be done throughout play interactions and the adult needs to be skilled at knowing when to model, how much to model, and when to allow the child to try (and often fail).

Modelling can take place in a variety of ways. Some examples are:

- Drawing a picture to illustrate your thinking.
- Making the item yourself and then getting children to copy. Use new vocabulary as you work through the model and at the end, check for understanding, asking questions about the order of the task, what came next and why particular materials were used. Sum up the process before letting the children move on.
- Demonstrating how to play in an area by playing alongside.
- Providing keyword cards on the table to support writing sentences. Use these when writing your own sentence to show children how to use them.

Modelling is the time to introduce new vocabulary as your actions will reinforce the meaning of the word. Children should be encouraged to say the words and use them as they play. An example would be introducing the word 'knead' while making dough. The adult needs to say the word and demonstrate or explain, for example, 'I am going to knead my dough. Can you knead your dough by pushing it like this?'

Metacognitive talk is an approach to modelling when playing alongside children. This is a strategy where the adult models the steps to solve a problem by narrating each step as they work through them. This is most useful for problem-solving or logic tasks, for example, when building a vehicle. The narrative will not involve the child, but will be said out loud, as the steps are done.

> 'I want to make a fire truck ... what do I need to make a fire truck? Wheels! Yes, I need wheels and I think a fire truck has four wheels. That is two on each side. I need an axle to hold them together. Let me find two sets of wheels on axles ... .'

Children will begin to contribute to this dialogue or listen and watch as the adult models each step.

If a task is to have a specific outcome, then providing an image or example of the finished product is important for children to know what they are aiming for. An example of this may be making a Diva lamp or writing in a Mother's Day card. If you have the task in the continuous provision, the completed model can act as a guide for the children, who can attempt to deconstruct the process in order to achieve the outcome.

Scaffolding is providing support to allow a child to accomplish more than they could without the scaffold. For the same reasons described above for modelling, young children need a great deal of scaffolding, supporting small and incremental steps. Modelling can provide a scaffold, especially if it is written or made and left out for children to see. If children are unable to complete a task independently, they need more scaffolds and stronger modelling.

CHAPTER 3
RESEARCH AND PERSPECTIVES

Being research-informed is an increasingly familiar concept for teachers. The act of being persistently curious about education and the specialist area in which you trained is important for driving your own professional development. As a teacher, you should strive to continually challenge your thinking and develop the habit of reflecting on your practice. Every teacher should be constantly asking questions about how we can improve teaching and learning for the children we work with.

Research-informed practice

Key takeaway

- Take control of your own continuous professional development by absorbing yourself in early years research.

Research is highly accessible due to organisations such as the Chartered College of Teaching, the Centre for Research in Early Childhood (CREC) and the Education Endowment Foundation (EEF). These organisations have allowed research to be more accessible to teachers and practitioners and have encouraged school improvement to be based on empirical findings.

Schools are becoming more skilled at asking questions about evidence, and about making conscious, informed decisions about what will improve outcomes for children. Teachers are more able to understand quantitative and qualitative data, and immerse themselves in discussion and debate about research and evidence.

Being research-informed means you consider how using research can develop your knowledge and your teaching and learning strategies. It helps to develop skills to identify which practices are ineffective. It helps develop reflective skills that question why we are doing the things we do in education, and questions whether things could be done in a more effective way. Using research-informed strategies will save you time as you engage in practice that has been empirically demonstrated to work.

As an early years teacher in the UK, you will have access to some leading research and be able to follow some highly inspirational research schools.

Refer to the extra resources at the end of this book to get a brief overview of some of these centres of excellence.

The remainder of this chapter highlights some influential research and tools in the early years sector. Much of this research has been conducted in the UK.

ECERS

Key takeaway

- ECERS is a tool to help assess the quality of your environment.

ECERS stands for Early Childhood Environment Rating Scale. The assessment tool started as a single book that was then developed into a family of documents (ECERS-3, ITERS, ECERS-E, SACERS-U) that meets the needs of different types of settings.

ECERS is a standardised tool designed to assess the quality of early childhood education and care environments. It is often used by educators, researchers and policymakers to evaluate the quality of early years programmes and their environment, and aims to highlight areas in which to make improvements.

The ECERS assesses various aspects of the learning environment, including space and furnishings, personal-care routines, language and literacy activities, and interactions between adults and children. The scale was designed as a culmination of early years research findings and so is well grounded in validated research.

It is advised that the ECERS assessment be completed alongside a person who has been trained in the scale. However, the ECERS is readily available to buy online. Completing an ECERS annually is a great way to ensure your environment is meeting children's needs.

REPEY

Key takeaway

- The REPEY study details the aspects of early years teaching that support greatest progress.

REPEY stands for Researching Effective Pedagogy in the Early Years. This study (2002) found that children made more academic and social progress when they had early education experiences that demonstrated the following:

- Adults have warm, responsive relationships with children.
- Adults and children were involved in high-quality interactions including sustained shared thinking.
- Setting has clear educational goals and planning.
- Staff have recognised early years qualifications.
- Trained teachers are among the staff.
- Parents are supported in being involved in children's learning.

Reflecting on these areas will support your development of a high-quality setting. It is worth spending time learning more about high-quality interactions and sustained shared thinking. This is discussed in more detail in the section on SSTEW later in this chapter.

EPPE

Key takeaway

- EPPE is a highly influential piece of research that evidences the impact on children of attending high-quality early years settings, and the marked impact this can have on disadvantaged children.

The Effective Provision of Pre-School Education (EPPE) study was completed in 2004. It is an influential, longitudinal-research project that aimed to investigate the impact of early childhood education and the factors that contribute to children's educational and developmental outcomes as they progress through primary and secondary school. The study followed a large group of children from 3 to 16 years of age. The study examined various dimensions of children's experiences, including the quality of early childhood education, family background, school factors, teaching practices, and children's cognitive, social and emotional development. One of the primary goals of the EPPE study was to investigate the impact of early education on children from disadvantaged backgrounds. It aimed to provide insights into how early interventions can help mitigate the effects of socioeconomic inequalities.

The findings of the EPPE study have had significant policy implications in the UK and beyond. The research provided valuable insights into the importance of high-quality early childhood education and the need for interventions that support children's development from an early age. The study's results have contributed to shaping early childhood education practices and policies, as well as discussions about the value of investing in early education to promote positive long-term outcomes.

A summary of the findings:

1. **Enhancement of all-round development:** Attending pre-school is associated with improved overall development in children when compared to those who do not attend pre-school.
2. **Duration matters:** Starting pre-school at an early age (under 3 years) is linked to better overall development.
3. **Benefits for disadvantaged children:** High-quality pre-school experiences are particularly beneficial for disadvantaged children. Diversity in social backgrounds within pre-school settings can enhance the benefits for disadvantaged children.
4. **Disadvantaged children attend for shorter periods:** Disadvantaged children tend to have shorter durations of pre-school attendance compared to more-advantaged groups.
5. **Variability in quality across settings:** Good-quality pre-school experiences can be found in various types of early years settings. Quality is often higher in settings that integrate both care and education, such as nursery schools.
6. **Staff qualifications:** Pre-school settings with staff who have higher qualifications tend to be better quality and contribute more to children's progress.
7. **Quality indicators:** Quality indicators include positive relationships between teachers and children, high-quality interactions, a trained teacher as the manager, and a substantial number of trained teachers among the staff.
8. **Balanced focus on educational and social development:** Pre-schools that prioritise both educational and social development equally tend to facilitate better overall progress in children.
9. **Effective pedagogy:** Effective teaching methods in pre-school include interactive teaching approaches, creating instructive learning environments, and promoting sustained shared thinking to extend children's learning.

The EPPE study has been widely cited and referenced in academic literature, policy documents and discussions about early childhood education and development. It has provided valuable evidence on the impact of early education experiences on children's later success in school and beyond, highlighting the critical role that quality early childhood education plays in shaping lifelong outcomes.

SEED

Key takeaway

- SEED is an ongoing piece of research. It is worth keeping track of the developments of this research as it progresses.

The Study of Early Education and Development (SEED) is a longitudinal study that involves interviews with parents when their child is 2, 3 and 4 years old. It is accompanied by assessments of children's cognitive, language and social development. The aim of the project is to offer the government (DfE) empirical insights into the effectiveness of early years education and the long-term advantages of funding for early years education. It has a specific focus on free early education for 2-year-olds.

Findings have not had a marked impact on school-based provision, as the focus was on funded education for 2-year-olds. However, the project has been extended to 2029 and so it may be worth revisiting this research as it continues to develop.

Sustained shared thinking and SSTEW

Key takeaways

- Sustained Shared Thinking and Emotional Wellbeing (SSTEW) is an assessment tool that will help you to understand the quality of the sustained shared thinking happening in your classroom.

'Sustained shared thinking' is described as an episode in which two or more individuals 'work together' to resolve a problem, clarify a concept, evaluate activities and extend a narrative. Both parties need to contribute to the thinking, and that thinking should be developed and extended (Siraj-Blatchford et al., 2002).

Sustained shared thinking can be characterised as moments when both you and a child are fully engaged, whether in conversation or an activity, driven by genuine curiosity to explore and discover more together.

These interactions provide significant chances for the practitioner to gain insights into a child's perspective. They unveil valuable information about the child, encompassing aspects like cognitive growth, schemas and self-esteem. Additionally, the child may acquire knowledge in areas such as social engagement, skill acquisition, creative thinking, grasping cause and effect, and factual learning.

The key features of sustained shared thinking are that the adult and child are working together on an intellectual task or a task that demands deep thinking. The process of sharing the experience is cognition, and engagement is extended beyond what the child could achieve alone.

In sustained shared thinking, you will observe the following:

- Conversation will be at the child's level of development and not adult speak.
- Questions should be natural and posed by both participants. Questions are usually open ended, and modelling is not forced.
- Positive body language. The adult will be at the child's height and the focus of both will be on the task or investigation.
- The adult will have a genuine interest in what the child is saying and doing. They will give their whole attention to the interaction and understand its importance.

The SSTEW scales were written to support practitioners to evaluate the quality of their sustained shared thinking. The scales build on the model used in ECERS-R and ECERS-E/ITERS-R as a tool to assess the quality of the interactions occurring between the adults and the children. The scale is presented in a similar way to the ECERS as a seven-point scale based on five specific areas of interaction.

1. Building trust, confidence and independence.
2. Social and emotional wellbeing.
3. Supporting and extending language and communication.
4. Supporting learning and critical thinking.
5. Assessing learning and language.

Having a go at the SSTEW is a great way to identify the strengths and areas for development of your interactions. This tool is available online. It is a good tool for self-reflection, but also for designing CPD that accurately reflects the training needs of the adults in your class.

Communication and language development

Key takeaways

- Speaking and listening ability is a strong determinator of end-of-school outcomes.
- Children with weaker communication need support to improve communication from the start of school.

The ability to communicate effectively is an essential component for any child to be able to access a school curriculum, and to be able to have a successful school experience. Children with poor communication skills run the risk of performing poorly academically, having low confidence and struggling to socialise with peers. A report by Hartshorne (2006) highlights that there are two groups of children who have speech, language and communication needs (SLCN).

1. Around 10% of children with SLCN have long-term and persistent difficulties.
2. A much greater percentage (50%) on school entry have transient difficulties that will resolve with the right support.

Müller (2022) supports the notion of six principles of language development. It is important that teachers have a good understanding of these principles so they can embed them within their pedagogy and practice.

Six principles of language development

1. **Children who hear more language develop it more quickly.** Being immersed in language is vital to developing an understanding of language patterns and language purpose. Young children need to be surrounded by language constantly. Children need to hear language in a variety of ways (such as songs, rhymes and stories) and for a variety of purposes (such as giving instructions, sharing news and problem-solving).
2. **Children develop vocabulary best in an area that interests them.** It is important to observe and spend time with children to know their passions and interests. You should then plan enhancements that will extend and support these interests. This is the time to introduce new vocabulary.

3. **Interactions support language development.** An interaction is a conversation and a shared experience. It is when adults play with children, rather than instruct them. You need to make time to play with the children every day. Interactions provide opportunities to scaffold language with modelling of correct sentence structure and vocabulary.
4. **Learning in context sticks.** Introducing new vocabulary in a context that is meaningful is much more impactful than learning vocabulary out of context. For example, learning names of shapes when building with blocks will stick more than doing a worksheet.
5. **Diverse language structures and words support language development.** Children who are learning EAL should continue to speak in their home language. Other tools, such as gestures, help support vocabulary development. Children should hear complex and academic vocabulary, such as the real names of dinosaurs.
6. **Vocabulary and grammar are developed mutually.** Vocabulary teaching should be embedded in correct grammatical sentences, not in isolation via word lists.

Intentional teaching

Key takeaway

- Intentional teaching is about carefully planning and reflecting on all aspects of the environment, pedagogical approaches and interactions, to support children's learning.

Studies into the effectiveness of interactions, and the quality of teaching in early years, has led to the development of the term 'intentional teaching'. It is a concept developed and explored in detail in settings in Australia and New Zealand.

Intentional teaching is the ongoing reflection on your actions and how they contribute to children's learning. It demands a conscious understanding and a mindful, calculated and purpose-driven approach to teaching methods. Being intentional applies to various aspects of decision-making, encompassing curriculum, relationships and direct teaching. It means actively planning, and acting with specific goals or outcomes for children's learning in mind so that you can select the most appropriate ways to interact and extend children's thinking and development. The idea of intentional teaching is somewhat in contrast to the notion of free-flow and exploratory play, where there is minimal adult control of either the learning objectives or the outcomes.

Intentional teaching is a fluid and evolving decision-making process that encompasses both premeditated activities and impromptu reactions to children's evolving curiosities. Teaching actions and engagements require ongoing adaptation to align with children's reactions and their present skill levels. This adaptation is crucial for advancing the teachers' goals and learning objectives.

Intentional teaching requires a variety of teaching methods, a good understanding of how young children learn and insights into each child's learning capacity. Teachers need to develop skills at identifying children's intentions and interests, allowing them to design learning opportunities that are collaboratively built instead of solely influenced by the teacher. A collaborative construction is more than learning alongside children; it requires teachers to engage in sustained shared thinking and develop a range of skills for inquiry, and critical and creative thinking.

An intentional teacher will do the following:

- Plan learning opportunities following observations that will use a variety of resources and approaches, e.g. adult directed to child initiated.
- Design and organise the environment to ensure children can access resources that will support and extend their learning in specific areas.
- Create situations that will challenge children's learning and design interactions that will scaffold learning and develop higher-order thinking skills.
- Decide which pedagogy to use and at what time, e.g. modelling, sustained shared thinking, child-initiated learning, questioning.

Interactive reading

Key takeaway

- Interactive reading is one tool to be used alongside phonics and reading to children, to develop reading skills and a love of books.

Interactive reading is the process of encouraging children to be actively involved in the reading of books. This is a different task to reading a book to a child, where they sit quietly and listen to the narration.

When doing interactive reading, the adult considers and plans for opportunities to engage the child, or small group of children, to become an active participant. This may be done by asking questions of the pictures or asking questions about the characters or storyline.

The adult will consider a prompt to draw children's attention to the element of the story to support the interaction. This could be done in several ways such as:

- Saying half a sentence and encouraging children to complete it. This works especially well with well-known stories and repetitive phrases.
- Pointing out part of a picture and modelling a comment about it, leaving time for children to add their own comments.
- Posing open-ended questions such as, 'I wonder why …'. These questions can extend thinking beyond simple recall, and aim to deepen the understanding of the story, the characters and the themes of the story.
- Discussing connections between the story and real life.
- Encouraging predictions about what might happen next.

The adult can use children's responses to model full sentences and use more ambitious vocabulary than the child would choose. For example, if the child points to the picture and says 'dog', the adult can reply, 'The dog is playing with the ball'.

Interactive reading fosters a positive relationship between the adult and the child, and establishes the groundwork for enduring reading practices and a passion for reading. This co-operative approach contributes to the child's cognitive, emotional and social growth, and helps develop reading for pleasure.

Collaborative talk

Key takeaway

- Planning for oracy development through collaborative talk will support children's confidence in speaking and listening.

Collaborative talk is an approach to developing oracy, and it supports communication skills, critical thinking, social interaction and a deep exploration of concepts. Sustained shared thinking may be a collaborative talk activity, but it could also be a specific activity planned on its own, rather than based on another activity.

Collaborative talk will be planned, with consideration given to the grouping of the children and the type of activity. The objective is to get all children talking and contributing to the discussion. Some types of activities that could be planned for collaborative talk are:

- **Problem-solving** – discussing a solution to a problem. For example, asking a small group of children what steps we could make towards helping Jack cut down the beanstalk.
- **Working with a peer** – setting tasks where children discuss the next steps, and work collaboratively. An adult supports the discussion and encourages turn-taking in contributing to the discussion.
- **Storytelling and performance** – an adult supports children to act out a role and speak the parts of the characters.
- **Sharing something from home with a small group**. This is like an old-fashioned show and tell, but in a small group, ensuring all children have opportunities to ask questions and contribute to the discussion.
- **Reflection on learning** – taking turns to discuss what children liked or didn't like about an activity they have done.
- **Peer teaching** – asking one child to teach another how to do a task. This collaborative activity will support speaking and listening.

A multitude of activities can support the development of oracy, but it needs to be a planned and considered element of the provision.

Use of gesture

Key takeaway

- Deliberate use of gesture will support children's developing speech and language.

Young children spend a lot of their time interpreting non-verbal body language, and gesture plays a crucial role in children developing an understanding of verbal language. Gesture supports comprehension when an adult points to an item and says its name. Likewise, pointing out items in a book will support the comprehension of the spoken story. Children will use gesture to express their needs, such as pointing to a child who has pushed them, or pointing to the toilet. If the adult confirms the understanding of this communication with a verbal reinforcement, children's understanding of the appropriate vocabulary will be contextualised.

Children will imitate gestures used by others. Telling stories or using songs and rhymes with actions will support understanding as children will first mimic the gesture, then attempt the words. Gesture will often precede speech both in young children and those learning EAL. Adults need to put high value on the gestures used as a form of communication, and to value and support their development. Gestures will not be culture- or language-dependent, so can be used as a form of international language for children who do not speak English yet. Gestures are multi-sensory which supports learning. Visual, auditory and tactile input enhances children's understanding and retention of language. Gestures are not reliant on complex grammatical structures, so are easier to use.

Some settings use forms of sign language, such as Makaton, to support learners. This is a more advanced form of gesture. However, gesture can be capitalised on without the need to train in sign language. An awareness of the importance of gesture will reinforce the drive to use this to support communication in an informed way.

CHAPTER 4
MISTAKES AND MISCONCEPTIONS

Managing the environment

Key takeaways

- You need to have very clear expectations on how the environment needs to be presented and stick to it. The children will pick up on these expectations.
- Clutter will have a negative impact on the learning environment. Maintain the mantra that **less is more**.
- For children to develop independence, it is vital that resources are well labelled and easy to access.

A beautiful, tidy and stimulating early years classroom is inspirational. It makes the fingers itch to play, explore and see what is in every corner. A cluttered, dirty and poorly presented space has the opposite effect.

It is a misconception to think that children need a lot of toys and resources to play with. Too many resources are impossible to manage and over time, the clutter builds. The room slowly becomes disorganised, and chaos ensues. Children need to be trained to put something away before they get out something new. This is a routine and expectation that needs to be set within the first few weeks of term. Many children may not have experienced the resources and opportunities open to them at school and so they need to be taught how to play with them, and how to put them away.

Children should be encouraged to treat resources with care and respect. Throwing or walking on toys should not be allowed. Children will quickly pick up the ethos of respecting equipment. Sticking rigidly to these expectations will pay dividends as the year progresses, as this means you can trust children with more-complex or fragile items (such as the tinker table) that offer an element of risky play.

At the beginning of the year, provide limited resources, and ensure children develop a good understanding of the expectations prior to adding more resources. You need to be very aware of your own items and make sure these are not building up and cluttering the environment. Cupboard tops should not be a space for your folders, planning, coffee cups, and pens and pencils. They should all be used for learning and your own items need to be stored neatly in one place.

Resources in your environment need to be clean, in good order and fit for purpose. This does not mean resources need to be new, or from an expensive shop. Many skilled early years staff find amazing resources that are upcycled. Natural resources such as pebbles, shells, pine cones and tree slices are all easy to amass, as are other loose-play articles such as wooden pegs, milk-bottle lids, cardboard tubes, corks and buttons. Furniture in settings can also include upcycled large cable reels for tables, pallets, and repurposed cupboards and dressers. Real-world items such as furniture, crockery, baskets, suitcases and lamps can provide texture, interest and a range of materials to help develop language. Families who are keen to clear children's bedrooms of barely used toys often willingly donate items to schools. While this is done in a spirit of supporting the school, these items are often unsuitable for school as they are not made for 30 children to be using them for 38 weeks a year. Be scrupulous over what you will accept and what you will politely refuse.

One aim of the learning environment is to promote and develop independence. All items need to be stored at a suitable height for children to access them independently. Trays or boxes of resources should be light enough for a child to carry and move them independently and so should not be too full. All boxes and trays should be clearly labelled with plain script and accompanied by an image. This is best done with photographs of the real item. Labels need to be secure, otherwise you will need to relabel things mid-year.

Be reflective of overstimulation in your environment. Consider the purpose of bright displays, coloured tables, contrasting coloured chairs, things dangling from the room and loud music. Try to ensure the environment is soothing and calm. Display backgrounds should be muted colours, allowing the items on display to be the focus of attention. The use of potted plants and soft furnishings of neutral colours will help soften a room. Fairy lights and tabletop lamps will provide softer lighting.

The mantra any teacher needs to adopt for their environment is **less is more**. Don't shy away from throwing away dated or broken resources. Teachers often store things with a plan to mend them later but the time constraints on schools and teachers mean this rarely happens. Only keep high-quality learning resources that children actively engage with. If a resource has not been used for a year, throw it away or rehome it.

There are many fantastic audit tools to ensure your environment is top quality. A Google search will find some, or you could engage in the internationally renowned ECERS audit. Alternatively, there is a simple audit provided in the extra resources at the end of this book. Doing audits regularly will help you to avoid falling into bad habits with the environment, and keeps you tuned in to what areas are working well and what areas need development.

Refer to the extra resources at the end of this book for examples of audits.

Attention

Key takeaways

- Young children have short attention spans. Whole-group sessions are difficult to manage and should always be short.
- Most direct teaching can be done in small groups. This offers rapid feedback to children and supports developing attention.

It is easy to underestimate how limited young children's concentration span is. Young children have fleeting attention spans. Attending to spoken language is cognitively demanding for all learners, but especially for younger children due to their rapidly developing brains. Many teachers and schools hold on to the notion that children are not learning unless they are focused on a teacher, who is talking at the front of the class. This approach is not supported by evidence, but these perceptions of what school, teaching and learning should look like are hard traditions to break. Many children who cannot concentrate will fidget, turn around, leave the carpet or touch their peers, but many will also sit still, looking at you, but be far away in their imaginations. Passive behaviour and active listening are different things that may look the same.

Keeping children on the carpet for any longer than 10–15 minutes is therefore counterproductive. Whole-class inputs need to be short and sharp, and children need to move on to experiential learning rapidly. Transitions need to be carefully planned, as young children are quickly distracted. Asking children to move from carpet to activity, from class to dining hall, from forest school to toilets offers hundreds of distractions. While it is important these routines are practised, they should not take up large parts of learning time. Correcting children who are distracted should be gentle as losing focus is not a choice for these children. Asking a 4-year-old child to stand in a line for five minutes while their peers get their coats on is unfair. Ask yourself how these routines can better reflect the developmental stage of these children. For example, can one adult wait outside, while another supports putting on coats inside, and children take themselves out? Many things we do in school, such as getting children to walk in lines, goes against what we know and understand about child development.

Aim to deliver as many directed sessions as possible in key groups. This means the children split into groups and go into an area of the room with an adult. Each adult then delivers the same input. For example, if the directed planning is to read a fact book, a group of 30 children is split among three adults, and they each read a book to 10 children. Key groups can be a familiar regular grouping, and these children will soon get used to moving into their key group. Delivering a session for 10–15 children will allow children to be closer to what the adult is sharing, to ask more questions and to have more immediate feedback.

Adults who are supporting children should always be active, so having teaching assistants (TAs) or nursery practitioners sitting on the carpet with children is not the best use of their time, unless they are actively supporting specific children. You may choose to set key groups reflective of developmental criteria, with developmentally younger children in a smaller group, allowing for more interaction. This allows the more mature group to have more demands put on them regarding questioning and time in the group.

Areas of provision

Key takeaway

- Zones and clear organisation will allow children to feel secure in where to find things.

There are many ideas in books and online as to what an early years classroom environment should contain. This will be influenced by things like the amount of space available and the resourcing and budget available. There is no right or wrong, as it is the delivery of the learning that matters. There are some areas that are standard in most early years classrooms such as blocks, carpet space, home corner, sand, water and an art area.

Refer to the extra resouces at the end of this book for an audit of suggestions for areas and what they are provided for.

The space between each area or zone needs to be defined in order to minimise distractions. This can be supported by children feeling enclosed, with furniture or barriers defining areas. Planning the room layout will ensure space is well used and neighbouring zones complement each other. For example, putting an activity that will naturally be noisy, such as role play or construction, next to the reading corner may cause disruption. A good indicator that the zones are not right, or that the environment is not engaging enough, is when children are running around a space, playing physical games and not settled in to an activity. Chaotic, noisy rooms indicate children who are not deeply engaged in play.

Zones need to be adapted in response to how the children are using them. If an area is never visited by the children, you need to consider why, and adapt it. Holding on to an area because the adults have spent a long time making it look beautiful does not justify keeping it. If the children do not use an area, it is not meeting their needs. Standing back and looking where the children are playing, and considering what resources they are accessing, is an important task that needs to be done regularly. Look at the children, listen to what they are doing. Do the children engage in mathematics in the maths area, or do they use the resources for other types of play? While it doesn't matter that children are flexible with the learning that occurs in an area, you need to be aware of the learning that is happening, and not just assume that the types of learning you had hoped would occur are happening.

Care does need to be taken in changing the layout of the classroom mid-year. Children will develop a sense of security in knowing where things can be found in the classroom. This familiarity allows them to return to areas to repeat and then extend their play. If areas change too frequently, this will be disrupted. The basic positioning of the zones should remain the same throughout the year, with only the resources available being amended, unless of course there is a real problem with the location of a zone, or if children are avoiding a part of the provision.

Managing support staff

Key takeaways

- Roles are less defined between adults in early years classrooms. Children will see you all as equal, and it is essential that all staff are prepared to do all jobs.
- Managing support staff is a complex task that takes confidence and experience.
- You need to have a clear vision of what you want to achieve to keep everyone on track. Staff will buy into your vision if it is comprehensive and well-articulated.

The best TAs and early years professionals are miracle workers. If you have staff in your class who understand early years pedagogy and practice, and support the class constantly with limited direction from you, hold on to them!

All adults in the early years classroom need to be prepared to muck in, work hard and do every element of care and education for the children, and this includes the teacher. Early years work is messy, it often has some unpleasant or unexpected elements, and frequently involves dealing with bodily fluids. Be very explicit with new staff that this is an expectation from all adults in the room. Lead by example and do your fair share of toilet duty, nappy duty, nose wiping and changing underwear.

Moving TAs from other year groups to early years cannot always be avoided and you may get a new TA who has never worked with young children before. If you find yourself in this position, you need to make time to induct this staff member into how your classroom operates, and source some training for them on child development, play and interactions.

Write rotas, ensuring all staff rotate through all areas of the provision. Make sure all adults work outside at some point in the day or the week, and make sure all staff are involved in observations, supporting play and in directed activities. Do not fall into the trap of having the teacher sit at the writing table every day, while the other staff do all the other areas of learning. All areas of learning need to be given equal importance.

Make sure the learning objective for directed activities is clear and that the TA understands the learning objectives. If the learning intention is not well understood by the adults, you run the risk of the task or activity becoming the focus, rather than the learning. Sharing planning with support staff is vital and it should be displayed on a wall where everyone can quickly refer to it. All staff should be able to articulate what children are learning in each activity (rather than what they are doing). Ask a member of the SLT to come in occasionally and test this out with staff by asking, 'What are the children learning here?'

Be prepared to direct staff when they go off task. For example, clearing and sorting the room during learning sessions needs to be minimised. Often, experienced staff can have very entrenched routines, and this will be a challenge if you want things changed. Stick to your plan, and gently guide staff until they understand their role.

You need to consider where support staff will be while you are leading whole-class sessions. For example, do you want them on the carpet, supporting individual children, or preparing other areas for continuous provision? Support staff are your most expensive resource and they need to be managed to ensure they are having a direct impact on children's learning and development. Using them for key groups is a great solution to this.

If you are struggling with the staff management in your room, seek support from the SLT. Staff management is complex and if you need some help, ask for it. A strong team will make for an efficient early years classroom, and it is fine to ask for help if you need it. It is common for young or new teachers to feel awkward directing older, more-experienced support staff. This gets easier with practice, and shying away from anxieties with managing staff will not help in the long run.

If you are lucky enough to be part of recruitment for support staff for early years, try and attract applicants with early years qualifications or experience working in a pre-school or nursery. This will save you time on induction as a person with experience will understand the nature of the work and have some knowledge of meeting young children's physical and learning needs.

Resisting top-down pressures

Key takeaway

- Develop a strong understanding of early years pedagogies and stand your ground defending them. Base your knowledge in research and evidence and then your knowledge will be easier to defend.

You may feel pressure from the SLT or the rest of the school to conform to pedagogies more suited to older children. Resist these pressures by reminding staff that the early years has a different curriculum and different pedagogies which should reflect the needs of young children.

Few Primary headteachers have been trained in or worked in early years classes. Often the SLT is uncertain about how to measure quality in a nursery or Reception classroom. The wholly different approach to pedagogy, environment, timetables and pupil groupings can be confusing for senior staff who need to make quick assessments of quality within the school. There is a tendency for people to refer to their comfort zones and this may lead to headteachers and the SLT pressuring early years staff to create more-formal early years classrooms, with desks for each child, and a whole-class, instructional-style teaching approach.

The best way to resist this pressure is to gently educate senior staff as to why the approach (as outlined in this book) is the way forward. Understanding research and being able to provide documents that support this thinking is essential when trying to explain your methods or propose new ideas to the SLT. As an early years teacher in any Primary school, you will be a minority. Confidence in your arguments for early years pedagogies will come with experience. You will need to have formed solid arguments for the approach for parents too.

Below are some questions you may want to spend some time formulating, and researching answers for, if you wish to inspire confidence in your approach.

- How do you ensure children learn if they are just playing?
- Why do children access the outdoors throughout the day, and not just at break and lunchtime like the rest of the school?
- When do you stop playing and start teaching?
- How can you make accurate assessments of children if you are not testing them?
- Why have you organised the classroom in this way?
- How do you differentiate the learning for children at different levels?
- How will they be ready for Year 1 if they play all the time?

Joining early years networks and attending CPD events will help you to find your tribe. This will stop you feeling isolated and help you develop your voice in defending early years pedagogy.

The rhythm of the year

Key takeaway

- Pinch points for early years will be different to the rest of the school. Find out what they are ahead of time so you can prepare for them.

Each sector of the education system has a rhythm of tasks and stresses. These are different in Reception and nursery to the rest of the Primary school.

Events	When	Details
Transition into Reception/ nursery	September	Transition should have started in June and July, and children should be well prepared for their transition. All of this early work will have an impact on children, but September is still a big month in early years. Children may start part-time or may start full-time, depending on your school routine. You will spend most of September teaching routines and expectations and are unlikely to be able to do much subject-content teaching as your focus will be mostly on communication and personal, social and emotional needs.
Baseline assessments	September–October	You will need to submit government baseline assessments within 6 weeks of children starting school. You will also do your own baseline observations of children within the first few weeks of them being in school so you can understand the starting points for the children. You will be spending considerable amounts of time just getting to know the children and understanding their passions, interests, fears and worries. →

Events	When	Details
Nativity/ Christmas (end-of-Autumn-term) performance	December	Most schools will hold a nativity or performance for the youngest children in the school. Children will have only been at school half a term before you need to start preparing for this event. It is a challenging event that will require a lot of work and effort, but the parents will love it.
Formative assessments and moderation events	April–June	You need to consider pulling all of your summative assessments together to create a formative judgement for the early learning goals (ELG). If you start this early, you can then target specific areas of learning, or give additional support to identified children if they are on the cusp of judgements.
Submission of data	June (end of)	Data needs to be submitted to local authorities around the end of June. Your school may be able to offer you administrative support with this.
Outings	May–July	A summer outing is a lovely event in the year. You want to time it when it is not too hot and get as many helpers as possible to support with this task.
Writing reports	May–June	Writing reports will take a considerable amount of time. Each school will have different dates for these, but they are usually produced for the Summer term.
Beginning transitions – contact families, supply school information and organise home visits	May–July	You need to allow a long time to plan, and then begin, transition work for next year. You will not be able to begin home visits or contact parents until school places are allocated to families, but you can begin to pull together the information you want to share, and to timetable when you will start visits or have stay-and-play dates.

On top of these events, you will have parent/teacher interviews, and other events bespoke to your school, such as school fêtes and firework events. It is worth knowing these ahead of time so you can plan your diary.

There may also be open days and opportunities the school has developed to promote your setting to parents to encourage them to apply for a place at your school. These need careful planning and may include elements of both in-school time for tours and open evening events. Be aware of the structure and timing of these and how much you are expected to contribute to or attend these.

CONCLUSION

Early years teaching is the most exciting phase of education, offering the unique privilege of witnessing rapid developmental growth in children. This swift progress requires teachers to continually adapt the environment and curriculum, ensuring nothing remains static for long. The child who enters nursery or Reception in September will be markedly different by July. Teachers must consistently raise the challenge and foster more-complex interactions each month. This dynamic environment is thrilling, and the rewards of working with young children are immense.

As this book draws to a close, it is evident that many of the topics introduced could be explored in much greater detail. This intentional brevity aims to avoid overwhelming teachers new to EYFS. The goal is to spark interest in these areas, encouraging further reading, research and learning. Engaging with wider early years networks is crucial for continually developing the skills, knowledge and experience necessary for a successful early years classroom.

If you are new to nursery or Reception, and are feeling overwhelmed by all that needs to be done, prioritise getting to know the children. Spend time playing and laughing with them and invest in building relationships with each child in your care. Discover their interests, sense of humour and challenges, and appreciate them as unique individuals. These relationships will be more meaningful to both you and the children than any single lesson. By investing this time and energy in the children, the learning will follow.

As we conclude this book, I present a final challenge: Should children stop learning through play at age 5? Are children developmentally so different between Reception and Year 1? Developmental research suggests otherwise. I urge schools, teachers and headteachers to consider whether Year 1 should be a play-based learning environment. If play is how children learn best, then this approach should be fully integrated into our curriculum whenever possible. Pose questions, challenge thinking and keep raising the profile of learning through play and developing challenging and exciting learning environments. Our children deserve it.

> *Play is the highest expression of human development in childhood, for it alone is the free expression of what is in a child's soul.*
>
> **Friedrich Froebel**

REFERENCES

Bradbury, A. and Swailes, R. (2022) *Early Childhood Theories Today*. Learning Matters. SAGE.

Bruner, J.S. (1996) *The Culture of Education*. Cambridge, Mass.: Harvard University Press.

Department for Education (2017) 'Development matters: Non-statutory curriculum guidance for the early years foundation stage'. Available from: www.gov.uk/government/publications/development-matters--2 [Accessed September 2025].

Early Education (2015) *Achieving excellence in the early years: a guide for headteachers*. The British Association for Early Childhood Education.

Early Years Coalition. (2021). 'Birth to 5 matters: non-statutory guidance for the Early Years Foundation Stage'. St Albans: Early Education. Available at https://birthto5matters.org.uk/wp-content/uploads/2021/04/Birthto5Matters-download.pdf [Accessed September 2025].

Education Endowment Foundation (EEF) (2018) 'Preparing for literacy: improving communication, language and literacy in the early years'. London: Education Endowment Foundation. Available from: https://educationendowmentfoundation.org.uk/education-evidence/guidance-reports/literacy-early-years

Education Endowment Foundation (EEF) (2020) 'Improving Mathematics in the early years and Key Stage 1: Guidance report'. London: Education Endowment Foundation. Available from: https://d2tic4wvo1iusb.cloudfront.net/eef-guidance-reports/early-maths/EEF_Maths_EY_KS1_Guidance_Report.pdf?v=1685389244 [Accessed September 2025].

Education Endowment Foundation (EEF) (2021) 'Teaching and learning toolkit: phonics'. London: Education Endowment Foundation. Available from: https://educationendowmentfoundation.org.uk/education-evidence/teaching-learning-toolkit/phonics [Accessed September 2025].

Education Endowment Foundation (EEF) (2023) 'Parental engagement'. London: Education Endowment Foundation. Available from: https://educationendowmentfoundation.org.uk/early-years/toolkit/parental-engagement [Accessed September 2025].

Education Scotland (2019) 'Schemas: learning through play' Available from: https://education.gov.scot/parentzone/learning-at-home/schemas/ [Accessed March 2023].

Fisher, J. (2016) *Interacting or interfering? Improving interactions in the early years*. Maidenhead: Open University Press.

Gill, T. (2007) *No Fear. Growing up in a risk adverse society*. Online. Available at: https://timrgill.files.wordpress.com/2010/10/no-fear-19-12-07.pdf [Accessed September 2025].

Harms, T., Clifford, R.M. and Cryer, D. (2014) *Early Childhood Environment Rating Scale*, 3rd ed. (ECERS-3). New York, NY: Teachers College Press.

Hartshorne, M. (2006) 'The cost to the nation of children's poor communication'. Research report. I CAN Charity.

International Association for Steiner/Waldorf Early Childhood Education (n.d.) Homepage. Available from: https://iaswece.org/home/ [Accessed September 2025].

International Children's Mathematics Research Network (n.d.) Homepage. Available from: www.childrens-mathematics.net/ [Accessed September 2025].

Laevers, F. (n.d.) Leuven scales for involvement and well-being. Available from: https://expertisecentrum.cego.be/team/ferre-laevers/?lang=en [Accessed June 2023].

Melhuish, E., Gardiner, J. and Morris, S. (2021) 'Study of Early Education and Development (SEED): impact study on early education use and child outcomes up to age three'. Research report. July 2017: revised November 2021. Available from: https://assets.publishing.service.gov.uk/government/uploads/system/uploads/attachment_data/file/1034423/SEED-Age_3_RESEARCH_REPORT.pdf [Accessed September 2025].

Müller, L.-M. (2022) 'Six principles of language development and how to support them in early childhood settings'. Research summary. Chartered College of Teaching.

National Centre for Excellence in the Teaching of Mathematics (NCETM) (n.d.) Homepage. Available from: www.ncetm.org.uk/ [Accessed September 2025].

NHS (n.d.) 'Physical activity guidelines for children (under 5 years)'. Online. Available from: www.nhs.uk/live-well/exercise/physical-activity-guidelines-children-under-five-years/ [Accessed September 2025].

Sherrington, T. and Caviglioli, O. (2020) *Teaching Walkthrus: Five-step guides to instructional coaching*. Woodbridge: John Catt Educational Ltd.

Siraj, I., Kingston, D. and Melhuish, E. (2015) *Assessing Quality in Early Childhood Education and Care: Sustained Shared Thinking and Emotional Well-being (SSTEW) Scale for 2–5-year-olds provision*. Stoke-on-Trent: Trentham Books.

Siraj-Blatchford, I., Sylva, K., Muttock, S., Gilden, R. and Bell, D. (2002) 'Researching effective pedagogy in the early years'. Institute of Education University of London. Department of Educational Studies University of Oxford. Queen's Printer.

Sylva, K., Melhuish, E., Sammons, P., Siraj-Blatchford, I. and Taggart, B. (2004) 'The effective provision of pre-school education (EPPE) project'. DfE.

Vygotsky, L.S. (1978) *Mind in Society: the development of higher psychological processes*. Cambridge, Mass.: Harvard University Press.

Zosh, J.M., Hopkins, E.J., Jensen, H., Liu, C., Neale, D., Hirsh-Pasek, K., Solis, L. and Whitebread, D. (2017) 'Learning through play: a review of the evidence' (white paper). The LEGO Foundation, DK.

EXTRA RESOURCES

1. Glossary

Early years glossary

2. Resource ideas

Resource ideas for areas of learning

3. Observations

Narrative observation example

Short observation example

Time sample observation example

The Leuven Scale for Well-being

The Leuven Scale for Involvement

Photo observation example

4. Audits

Indoor environment audit

Outdoor environment audit

5. Organisations and researchers

Organisations to follow

Researchers and authors to follow

6. Plan examples

Long-term plan example

Medium-term plan example: Personal, Social and Emotional Development (PSED)

Medium-term plan example: Understanding the World (UW)

Knowledge organiser example: Space

Knowledge organiser example: Minibeasts

Sample timetable for Reception

Sample timetable for nursery

Continuous provision and enhancements plan example (nursery)

Continuous provision and enhancements plan example (Reception)

Weekly planning: Maths

Weekly planning: Literacy

Weekly planning: Topic work

1. Glossary

Early years glossary

adult interactions	How an adult interacts with a child to support and develop learning. These can be high-quality or poor-quality.
adult led	The adult is driving the learning and the outcome of the lesson. The adult has a particular focus in mind and is controlling the session.
attachment	The relationship between the child and the adult. The type of attachment reflects the parent-to-child relationship. There are several forms of attachment which may affect how a person forms relationships and their behaviour.
benchmarks	Statements about where something should be at what stage. For example, what is expected at stages of learning for a 4-year-old.
cardinality	The quantity of things.
characteristics of effective learning	A term used in the EYFS (England) to describe behaviours children use to learn. They are Playing and Exploring, Active Learning, and Creating and Thinking Critically.
child-centred learning	Putting the child in the centre of the learning. Adults facilitate learning rather than telling children what to do; learning that is driven by children's interests.
child-initiated play	Play that children lead themselves.
co-construction	When the adult and child/children come together to create learning jointly as equals. May be known as partnership learning.
cognitive	Process of thinking, memory and reasoning.
continuous provision	See *child-centered learning.*
cruising	A way that babies may learn to move before walking. This involves using furniture to help move around while side stepping.

cultural capital	Experiences and opportunities children have had in their lives that have shaped their development.
developmental pathway	The expected path a child will take when developing in an area.
digital literacy	The ability to use technology with purpose.
early intervention	A programme put in place to support child development.
Early Learning Goals (ELG)	Summative assessment for the EYFS (England) prior to moving to (Key Stage 1) KS1. This data is submitted to government.
Early Years Foundation Stage (EYFS)	A document used in England to set the curriculum for the learning, development and care of children from birth to 5 years of age.
enabling environments	Planned environment that is well resourced to support learning and develop independence that is nurturing and safe.
evidence	Materials that support knowledge of a child, usually used in regards to assessments.
fine motor skills	The physical development of the coordination of the small muscles to allow fine movements. Mostly involves manipulation of small items with hands and fingers.
focused observation	A long, planned observation of a child, usually in play. Same as a narrative observation.
forest school	Sessions in a woodland, led by a qualified forest school leader.
free flow	The opportunity for children to move freely between areas, often indoors and outdoors, and to choose to play with what interests them.
good level of development (GLD)	An assessment measure that describes the expected standards of development for children moving to KS1 in England in each area of learning.
gross motor skills	Coordinated movements that involve the large muscle groups in activities, such as running, jumping, throwing and catching.

heuristic play	Play that is centred around everyday objects (rather than toys). Most often provided for babies and toddlers and may include items like pots, pans, spoons, containers and brushes.
intentional teaching	Use of knowledge, judgement and expertise to create learning experiences and the ability to recognise teaching moments.
interdisciplinary learning	Making links and connections to areas of the curriculum – teaching the whole child.
key person	One adult linked to a small group of children. The key person forms a caring and secure relationship with this group and is a key point of contact for parents.
learning environment	Planning and creation of an environment that supports learning through play.
learning through play	Understanding that a play environment supports learning.
loose-parts play	Play with a selection of items that can be used in multiple ways, e.g. planks of wood, buttons, bottle tops, reels. These items are open ended and not specifically toys.
mathematical graphics	Marks made to explore mathematical thinking and to show ideas.
Montessori method	Child-centred method of education developed by Maria Montessori in the 1900s.
narrative observation	A long, planned observation of a child, usually in play. Observes interactions, attention, interests and conflicts for a child. It is the same as a focused observation.
non-verbal	Communication that occurs without spoken words. May be used as a description of a learner who cannot communicate orally.
open-ended play	Play that has no specific purpose or end goal and is driven completely by the children engaged in the play.
palmar grip	Grasping things with the whole palm rather than fingers.
partnership working	Parents and a school working closely together to support children's progress and development.

pedagogy	The method and practice of teaching.
phonics	A method for teaching reading by breaking down words into individual sounds.
practitioner	A person who works in an early childhood setting. Describes a variety of qualifications from none to degree level.
prime areas	Three core area of the EYFS curriculum: Communication and Language (CL); Physical Development (PD); Personal, Social and Emotional Development (PSED).
profile	Record of a child's progress and outcomes over a set period.
pro-social approach	Opposite of antisocial. It is an approach to supporting a person's behaviour with a concern for their rights, feelings and welfare.
ratio	Number of adults relative to the number of children as defined as a legal requirement in the UK. The ratio of adult to child varies depending on the age of the children.
Reggio Emilia	Province in Italy where the Reggio Emilia approach was developed. This is an educational philosophy that promotes a child-centred, self-guided curriculum with a focus on experiential learning.
schemas	Repeated actions and behaviours displayed by young children as they explore and develop an understanding of the world around them.
self-directed learning	Learning led by the child.
self-regulation	The ability for a person to manage emotions in a socially acceptable way in response to different demands of the world around them.
sensory	Use of physical senses, e.g. touch, smell, taste, hearing, sight and proprioception.

short observation	Quick note of a learning event for an individual. Can be a short note or a photo. May be done electronically using specific early years software, or on paper. Used to note achievements and to develop planning.
spatial awareness	An awareness of objects in space around the body and the body's position in that space.
specific areas	The areas of the EYFS curriculum that are not prime areas. They are: Literacy (L); Mathematics (M); Understanding the World (UW); Expressive Arts and Design (EAD).
subitising	The ability to look at a small number of objects and recognise the quantity without counting them.
sustained shared thinking	When two or more people work together to do a task or solve a problem. Each participant has an active role in the activity.
synthetic phonics	Learning sounds in English; putting them together and breaking them down to read and spell words.
tripod grip	Holding a pencil correctly between thumb and two fingers when writing.
tummy time	Time for babies to play on their tummies. Important for the development of neck and spine muscles.

2. Resource ideas

Resource ideas for areas of learning

Maths			
Number and counting	**Measuring**	**Sorting**	**Shape and pattern**
Dice of different types Numicon Counters Money Five frame and ten frame Dominoes Track board games Spinners Playing cards Number lines 100 square – big and small Blocks Large number tracks and grids on the floor to jump on Number fans Board games, such as snakes and ladders Base ten sets Coins	Tape measures Rulers Sand timers Balance scales Bathroom scales Different-sized containers and jugs Spirit levels Stopwatches Measuring scales Measuring worms Jugs with volume markers Measuring spoons Measuring wheels Pedometers	Pebbles Pine cones Buttons Coloured pencils and matching coloured tins Animal cards Sorting dishes and items in colours Beads Ten frames Sorting trays	Blocks – large and small Textured shapes 3D/2D shapes Polydron Peg boards Shape sorters Biscuit cutters Puzzles Jigsaws Train tracks Foam shapes Numicon Shape gel tiles Shape sorter

Number songs and rhymes	Books	Outdoors	Time
Five Current Buns *Five Little Speckled Frogs* *Ten Fat Sausages* *Five Little Ducks* *Once I Caught a Fish Alive* *One, Two, Buckle my Shoe* *The Ants Go Marching* *Ten in the Bed* Finger puppets Nursery rhyme books	*The Gingerbread Man* *The Enormous Turnip* *How Many Legs?* *The Very Hungry Caterpillar* *The Doorbell Rang* *How Many Jelly Beans?* *One Mole Digging a Hole* *How Big is a Million?* *The Perfect Fit* *Ten Little Fingers and Ten Little Toes*	Skittles Beanbags Acorns Pine cones Pulleys Weather station Sundial Maps Wall number line Stopwatches Sand timers Chalk Rubber number mats Number pebbles Numbers on the floor (markings such as number tracks and hopscotch)	Real clocks – digital and analogue Toy clocks – digital and analogue Diaries and calendars Watches Sand timers Stopwatches Visual timetable History timelines Sundial Pictures of events in history, e.g. Victorian clothes

Communication and Language	
Speaking and listening	**Reading and comprehension**
Talking cans Walkie-talkies Headphones and recorded stories Microphones Old phones/toy phones Dens/tents Talking tubes Board games Puppets Talking clipboards	Fiction books Fact books Rhyme and poetry books Fact cards to support topics around the room Instruction cards for areas such as art and construction Recorded stories Puppets Small world story characters Beanbags and cushions Comics Maps Keyword cards

Expressive Arts and Design	
Media and materials	**Performance**
Paints (watercolour, powder, ready-mixed)	Recorded music to play, e.g. CDs
Easels	Microphones
Brushes	Stage area
Sponges	Instruments
Tape (masking and Sellotape)	Ribbons
Scissors	Open-ended costumes, e.g. hats
Clay	Dressing-up costumes
Dough	
Crayons	
Trays (paint mixing and larger)	
Felt-tip markers	
Pencils	
Glue sticks and PVA glue	
Glue spreaders	
Craft sticks	
Straws	
Aprons	
String	
Craft resources, e.g. pom poms, feathers, pipe cleaners, glitter, googly eyes, sequins	
Rollers	
Paint dabbers	
Stencils	
Pegs	
Felt and fabric	
Wool	
Paper and card (coloured and plain)	

<table>
<tr><th colspan="3">Personal, Social and Emotional Development</th></tr>
<tr><th>Emotions and self-regulation</th><th>Attention</th><th>Health</th></tr>
<tr><td>Images of different emotions
Puppets
Mirrors
Emotions games
Books on emotion themes
Teddies
Worry monster
Photos from home
Sensory toys: glitter wands, light-up resources, textured balls, stretch toys, infinity mirror</td><td>Sand timers
Watches
Ear defenders
Squishy fidget toys
Textured cushions
Weighted lap toy</td><td rowspan="3">Models of body parts, e.g. teeth, eye
Toy foods
Healthy eating posters
Food puzzles
Healthy food posters
Healthy eating games
Teeth cleaning boards (brush and teeth image)
Dentist/doctor play sets
Books about topics such as visiting the dentist, going into hospital</td></tr>
<tr><th>Personal needs and independence</th><th>Friendships</th></tr>
<tr><td>Handwashing posters
Potty/toilets that are easy to access
Books on toileting
Visual timetable
Now and next boards</td><td>Puppets
Conversation cubes
Friendship bench</td></tr>
</table>

Understanding the World	
The world and places	**Jobs/people who help us**
Globe Maps Books about other countries and cultures Clocks Fossils Binoculars Weather station Science books Posters/images of other places Gardening tools	Profession dressing up – nurse, firefighter, doctor, etc. Vehicles of different professions – police car, fire engine, etc. Books of different jobs Fact cards about different jobs Puzzles of different professions Finger puppets Doctor's kit, dentist's kit, builder's kit, police kit
Technology	**Diversity**
Laptops Phones Watches Bee-bots Typewriters Tills Toy scanners Tablets Torches Recordable buttons	Variety of small world people representing different ethnicities and disabilities Books with diverse representation Puppets Baby dolls of different skin colours and outfits

Physical Development	
Gross motor	**Fine motor**
Bikes Trikes Balance bikes Hoops Skipping ropes Crates Hopscotch Tunnels Doll's pushchair See-saw Gutters Balls Rackets Parachute Balance logs and planks Large blocks Tyres Den kits and tents Long ribbons and scarves Large spades in sand Large rollers Big brushes Brooms	Buttons/beads/sequins Tweezers and tongs Pens Pencils Marker pens Chalk Peg boards Sets of locks and keys, or nuts and bolts Stacking towers Syringes Droppers Threading and lacing kits Puzzles Fine paint brushes Fidget spinners Muffin trays for sorting small objects Finger puppets Playdough Gloop Shaving foam Scissors and glue (cutting and sticking) Spray bottles Washing line and pegs Variety of boxes and containers that need to be opened in different ways Busy board Paper clips Bulldog clips Sticky tape in a dispenser

Literacy	
Reading	**Writing**
Fiction books (picture books, comics) Non-fiction books (fact books, cookbooks, magazines) Rhyme and poetry books Fact cards to support topics around the room Recorded stories Phoneme display and cards Keyword cards Instruction cards for areas such as art and construction Magnetic letters Gel letters Leaflets Takeaway menus Maps Signs around the environment Magnetic letters and boards Signs featuring different languages Timetables Menus	Pens, pencils, crayons, marker pens Paint brushes Chalk Computers and tablets Modelled writing examples Keyword cards to copy Whiteboards Blackboards Paper and card Pads Notebooks Envelopes Sticky notes and labels Address books Diaries Touch screen whiteboards/tablets Post box Magic writer/magnetic writing Calendars Blank cards Blank zig zag and stapled books Pencil sharpeners Hole punch Rulers Scissors Clipboards Invitations

3. Observations

Narrative observation example

Date	Child	Observer
Observation:		
Reflections and next steps:		

Short observation example

Short observation	Short observation
Name Date Observer	Name Date Observer
Observation:	Observation:
PSED PD CL L M UW EAD	PSED PD CL L M UW EAD
Next steps:	Next steps:

Short observation	Short observation
Name Date Observer	Name Date Observer
Observation:	Observation:
PSED PD CL L M UW EAD	PSED PD CL L M UW EAD
Next steps:	Next steps:

Short observation	Short observation
Name Date Observer	Name Date Observer
Observation:	Observation:
PSED PD CL L M UW EAD	PSED PD CL L M UW EAD
Next steps:	Next steps:

Time sample observation example

No.	Time	Action, situation and area	Others present	Language	Further notes
1					
2					
3					
4					
5					
6					
7					
8					
9					
10					
Reflections and next steps:					

The Leuven Scale for Well-being

https://expertisecentrum.cego.be/leuven-scale-for-well-being/?lang=en

Level	Well-being	Signals
1	Extremely low	The child clearly shows signs of discomfort such as crying or screaming. They may look dejected, sad, frightened or angry. The child does not respond to the environment, avoids contact and is withdrawn. The child may behave aggressively, hurting him/herself or others.
2	Low	The posture, facial expression and actions indicate that the child does not feel at ease. However, the signals are less explicit than under level 1 or the sense of discomfort is not expressed the whole time.
3	Moderate	The child has a neutral posture. Facial expressions and posture show little or no emotion. There are no signs indicating sadness or pleasure, comfort or discomfort.
4	High	The child shows obvious signs of satisfaction (as listed under level 5). However, these signals are not constantly present with the same intensity.
5	Extremely high	The child looks happy and cheerful, smiles, cries out with pleasure. They may be lively and full of energy. Actions can be spontaneous and expressive. The child may talk to him/herself, play with sounds, hum, sing. The child appears relaxed and does not show any signs of stress or tension. He/she is open and accessible to the environment. The child expressed self-confidence and self-assurance.
Reflections and next steps:		

The Leuven Scale for Involvement

https://expertisecentrum.cego.be/leuven-scale-for-involvement/?lang=en

Level	Involvement	Signals
1	Extremely low	Activity is simple, repetitive and passive. The child seems absent and displays no energy. They may stare into space or look around to see what others are doing.
2	Low	Frequently interrupted activity. The child will be engaged in the activity for some of the time that they are observed, but there will be moments of non-activity when they will stare into space, or be distracted by what is going on around them.
3	Moderate	Mainly continuous activity. The child is busy with the activity but at a fairly routine level and there are few signs of real involvement. They make some progress with what they are doing but don't show much energy and concentration, and can be easily distracted.
4	High	Continuous activity with intense moments. The child's activity has intense moments and at all times they seem involved. They are not easily distracted.
5	Extremely high	The child shows continuous and intense activity revealing the greatest involvement. They are concentrated, creative, energetic and persistent throughout nearly all of the observed period.
Reflections and next steps:		

Photo observation example

Name	Date
Photo:	Context:
Reflections and next steps:	

4. Audits

Indoor environment audit

Given here is a list of suggestions of some areas you may want to provide in your indoor learning environment.

More ideas for resources can be found under **2. Resource ideas**.

Area	What this area may provide	What this area may contain	In place	Comments
Block area/ construction	Understanding of shape and concepts of construction Problem-solving and challenge	Blocks, boxes, 3D shapes, LEGO®, Duplo, wood slices		
Home corner	Language development, individual and cooperative play, imitating and pretending, stirring, filling, pouring, reacting events	Kitchen, plates, cups, utensils, chair, tables, dressing-up items, dolls, cooking tools, baking equipment, containers, soft furnishings (curtains, cushions)		
Writing/ mark-making table	A space to sit properly for writing and mark making Chairs of the right height and suitable tables	Clipboards, paper, pens, pencils, crayons, envelopes, felt-tipped pens, alphabet/phonics mats, name cards, keyword cards, whiteboards and pens, pads, Post-it notes, diaries		
Creative/art area	Colour mixing, creativity, construction skills	Paint, brushes, paper, glue, scissors, recycled materials (boxes and containers), feathers, sponges, string, items for sewing, easels, painting aprons		
Maths area	Exploring shape and number, measures, sorting, time, shape and pattern	Dice, numicon, counters, money, five frame and ten frame, dominoes, track board games, spinners, playing cards, number lines, 100 square (big and small), blocks, number fans, board games, base ten sets, tape measures, rulers, sand timers, scales, jugs		

Area	What this area may provide	What this area may contain	In place	Comments
Book corner	Reading for pleasure, language development	Books (fiction and fact), comics, maps, story props and puppets, sofa, cushions, rug, teddies, beanbags, recorded stories and headphones, word cards		
Carpet area	A large space for whole-group work, or for children to make large play such as construction and role play	Rug – one with marked spaces for sitting is helpful as children need to learn how to sit spaced out, not on top of each other or a long way apart		
Gross motor	Exercising big muscle groups, developing coordination and control	Tunnels, large blocks, long ribbons and scarves, beanbags and containers, balloons (to keep up in the air), large boxes (to hide in), doll's pushchair		

Area	What this area may provide	What this area may contain	In place	Comments
Fine motor	Exercising small muscle groups, developing coordination and control	Buttons/beads/sequins, tweezers and tongs, pens, pencils, marker pens, chalk, peg boards Sets of locks and keys, or nuts and bolts (real-life objects), stacking towers, syringes, droppers, threading and lacing kits, puzzles, fine paint brushes, fidget spinners, muffin trays for sorting small objects, finger puppets, playdough, gloop, shaving foam, scissors, glue Sticky tape in a dispenser, spray bottles, washing line and pegs, variety of boxes and containers that need to be opened in different ways, busy board, paper clips, bulldog clips		
Sensory	Opportunities to explore different senses of touch, smell, sight and hearing	Music, light table, lavender pouches, squeezy toys, gel pouches, shaving cream, cornflour, gloop, feathers, pom-poms		
Malleable	Developing hand strength, sensory opportunities, Expressive Arts and Design (EAD) opportunities	Clay, shaving foam, dough, tools, dough with items in it (such as seeds)		

Area	What this area may provide	What this area may contain	In place	Comments
Tinker table	Developing coordination and control, links to design technology, learning to use tools safely, learning to keep yourself safe, EAD opportunities	Saws, eye-protection goggles, nails, small hammers, wood, dowel, sticks, glue, wheels, screwdrivers, tape measures, pliers, vice		
Role play	Space and resources for dressing up and role play	Babies, pushchair, baby bed, table, chairs, plates, cups, utensils, pots and pans, dressing-up clothes with diverse representation, dressing-up tabards, doctor's kits, dentist's kits, builder's kits		
Water	Developing understanding of capacity and volume Developing coordination and control Sensory opportunities	Jugs, items that float and sink, buckets with holes, containers (metal and plastic), animals, nets, water spinners, syringes, pumps, boats, guttering		
Technology	To understand cause and effect and to be able to capture ideas and manipulate outcomes	PC, laptop, tablets, programmable toys, cash registers, phones, cameras, recordable buttons, remote-control toys, walkie-talkies, music player		

Area	What this area may provide	What this area may contain	In place	Comments
Den/places to hide	Language skills, construction skills, teamwork, sensory opportunities, problem-solving, negotiation skills, creative skills, mathematical concepts, engineering skills, physical development	Pegs, fabric, cushions, framework to peg fabric to, tarpaulins, rope, camo netting, blankets, yoga mats, carabiners, gaffer tape, bungee ropes		
Music area	To listen to and create music, or to respond to music with dance and movement To derive pleasure from music	CD player and CDs (or other form of device for accessing music), headphones, instruments, recording buttons		
Small world	To be able to use imagination to retell and create stories and to create landscapes and explore characters	Small figures (dinosaurs, animals, people, houses, boats, vehicles), branches, artificial grass, fabric, rocks and pebbles, tuff tray, shaving foam, glass pebbles, log slices, sand, small toy trees		
Cafe area	Taking responsibility for a task, waiting for your turn, language skills, social skills	Milk, fruit, child-friendly knives, chopping boards, cloths, spray containers (water only), bowls, plates		

Area	What this area may provide	What this area may contain	In place	Comments
Science and investigation area	Trial and error skills, exploration, scientific principles, curiosity, exploration	Batteries, bulbs, crocodile clips and wires, magnets, magnifying glasses, variety of natural items (such as pine cones and leaves), plant aquarium, classroom pets (such as stick insects or fish)		
Sand	Sand play on a smaller scale than outside Fine motor skill development in hands	Containers, jugs, spoons, small spades		
Space	Enough space between zones and furniture that adults and children can move freely, and health and safety is prioritised	Uncluttered pathways and consideration for mobility aids and those with reduced mobility Nothing stored in doorways and children understand not to leave things in areas people need to move through		
Handwashing and toileting	Pictorial reminders and good accessibility remind children to be hygienic and allow them to toilet independently	Easy to reach toilet paper, step (unless toilets are infant size), handrails, handwashing posters, liquid soap in a pump, enough room for an adult to get into the cubicle if the child needs help		

Outdoor environment audit

Given here is a list of suggestions of some areas you may want to provide in your outdoor learning environment.

The outdoors should not mirror the indoors. It should offer a different type of provision to indoors. If there is a water tray indoors, this may have small jugs that require more careful control. Outdoor water trays should allow for more mess – pouring from larger containers and using larger equipment to transport water, such as guttering.

More ideas for resources can be found under **2. Resource ideas**.

Area	What this area may provide	What this area may contain	In place	Comments
Sand	Gross motor development lifting heavy buckets Sensory opportunities	Spades, buckets, small rakes, small brooms, dumper trucks, diggers		
Water	Gross motor development and coordination lifting containers and pouring into different-width containers Sensory opportunities	Jugs, gutters, tubes, buckets, containers, scoops, nets, small-world toys (boats, ducks)		
Gross motor	Large space for children to do fast activities that support gross motor development	Bikes, trikes, balance bikes, hoops, skipping ropes, crates, hopscotch, beanbags, tunnels, see-saw, gutters, balls, rackets, parachute, balance logs and planks, large blocks, tyres, long ribbons and scarves		
Planting area	Areas for digging and planting, using tools, using large muscle groups, developing coordination	Compost, seeds, buckets, watering cans, hand tools		
Bikes and trikes	Opportunities to learn to ride a bike or trike and learn balance, coordination, control to speed up and slow down and change direction, collaboration to get around the track Develop strength and fitness	Bikes, scooters, a track to follow, road signs, obstacles (such as cones or tyres)		

Area	What this area may provide	What this area may contain	In place	Comments
Stage performance area	Performance skills, language skills, developing confidence, oracy	System for playing music, a stage, curtains that can be opened and closed, dressing-up items		
Making table	Creative investigation, problem-solving	Varieties of tape (masking tape, sticky tape), paper, card, clean recycled objects (boxes, tubes)		
Mud kitchen	Sensory opportunities, PSED, science	Compost, sand, mud, pots, containers, spoons, water, watering cans, cups		
Large loose parts	Construction skills, problem-solving, trial and error, team working, exercising large muscle groups and developing coordination	Pallets, gutters, tyres, large blocks, plastic pipes, large boxes, crates, spools, buckets, sticks		
Natural/wild space	A place to look for insects and other wildlife and to investigate different types of plants Awe and wonder, appreciation of nature, wellbeing	Bushes, pathways, woodlands, grassed areas, bug hotels, pooters, bark, logs		
Writing and mark making	This should comprise a variety of resources that will be moved around the outdoors and so may not be kept in one space as it may be when indoors	Sets of plastic tool trays holding clipboards, pens, pencils, whiteboards, whiteboard pens, notebooks, Post-it notes, sticky labels		

Area	What this area may provide	What this area may contain	In place	Comments
Construction area	Construction skills, problem-solving, trial and error, team working, exercising large muscle groups and developing coordination	Tape measures, hard hats, rulers, tyres, large planks, crates, fabric, sponge bricks, spanners, toy concrete mixer, builder's signs		
Den area	Language skills, construction skills, teamwork, sensory opportunities, problem-solving, negotiation skills, creative skills, mathematical concepts, engineering skills, physical development	Fabric, camo netting, pegs, framework to peg fabric to, tarpaulins, ground pegs, small hammers, rope, yoga mats, carabiners, gaffer tape, bungee ropes		
Areas of beauty	Awe and wonder, appreciation of nature, wellbeing	Flowers and plants in pots, water fountain, logs, ornamental grasses, variety of seating (such as loungers and cushions), arbours, sensory herbs and plants (e.g. lavender), smooth pebbles		
Weather station	Interaction with nature and the environment, understanding cause and effect, mathematical concepts of measuring	Sundial, thermometer, umbrellas, wellies, rain gauge, windsock, weather vane, small solar panel		

5. Organisations and researchers

Organisations to follow

Organisation	Webpage	What they do
Community Playthings	www.communityplaythings.co.uk/learning-library	Blogs and ideas for different areas of learning. Sell high-quality early years furniture and resources.
Education Endowment Foundation (EEF)	https://educationendowmentfoundation.org.uk/	Provides resources aimed at improving outcomes in schools and settings. Dedicated early years sections including an Early Years Toolkit.
Early Excellence	https://earlyexcellence.com/	Company that delivers CPD and consultancy in support of early years education. Early Excellence has an early years resources store that sells high-quality early years furniture and resources.
Early Education	https://early-education.org.uk/	Charity that delivers CPD for the early years workforce and runs campaigns advocating for early years. They publish books and a journal.
Chartered College of Teaching, Early Years Hub	https://chartered.college/	Articles about early years, by a mix of experts and practitioners, with an aim of developing pedagogy and thinking about early years.
Twinkl	www.twinkl.co.uk/	Resources (paid for) that may support topics and planning.

Organisation	Webpage	What they do
Early Years TV	www.earlyyears.tv/	Interviews with early years experts, discussing all things early years (paid for).
ABC Does	https://abcdoes.com/	Webinars on a variety of early years issues.
Centre for Research in Early Childhood (CREC)	www.crec.co.uk/	UK-based early childhood research.
Education Policy Institute	https://epi.org.uk/research-area/early-years-development/	An independent research institute that provides publications and research on education, including early years.
British Educational Research Association (BERA)	www.bera.ac.uk/	UK educational research.
***Early Childhood Environment Rating Scale* (ECERS)**	Can be purchased from Amazon: www.amazon.co.uk/Early-Childhood-Environment-Rating-ECERS-3/dp/0807755702	Provides an audit of the environment to help identify areas of focus.
Children's Mathematics Research Network	www.childrens-mathematics.net/childrens-mathematics-2/	Presents research and discussion about young children's mathematical development in an international context.
National Centre for Excellence in the Teaching of Mathematics (NCETM)	www.ncetm.org.uk	Provides articles and information for developing mathematics teaching, including early years.

Researchers and authors to follow

Researcher/author	Research and areas of interest and expertise
Professor Iram Siraj-Blatchford	A professor at the University of Oxford. She has been influential in many longitudinal research studies on early childhood, pedagogy, language development and early years leadership. The work on the EPPSE and REPEY studies had a marked impact on policy development within the UK.
Professor Kathy Sylva (OBE)	An Honorary Research Fellow and Professor Emeritus at the University of Oxford. Research in early childhood curriculum and assessment.
Professor Ferre Laevers	Professor in early years education, most well-known for the Leuven scale or Well-being scale. His theories are based on the importance of the early years setting in supporting and developing children's wellbeing. Using an assessment tool, such as the Leuven scales, can help to plan the environment or put in support for an individual child.
Professor Chris Pascal (OBE)	Established the CREC alongside Tony Bertram, and was involved in the British Association for Early Childhood Education (BAECE). Specialises in early childhood research and is president of the European Early Childhood Education Research Association (EECERA). Expertise in early childhood development and quality of early education services.
Professor Tony Bertram	Established the CREC with Chris Pascal. Editor-in-chief of the *European Early Childhood Education Research Journal*. Expertise in early childhood research, data and analysis for policy and practice in the early childhood sector.
Alistair Bryce-Clegg	Consultant and writer in early years. Has published articles and books about early childhood education and delivers training and CPD.

Researcher/author	Research and areas of interest and expertise
Dr Julie Fisher	An independent early years adviser and visiting professor at Oxford Brookes University. Has conducted research and written books about early years education (with a specialism in transitions) and play-based learning in KS1. Delivers CPD in a variety of areas.
Dame Cathy Nutbrown	Early childhood academic and professor at the University of Sheffield. Has conducted research and writings on qualifications in the early years sector. Editor-in-chief of the *Journal of Early Childhood Research*.
Edward Melhuish	Professor at the University of Oxford. Has contributed to many research projects in early years and to many social policy documents in the UK.
Pam Sammons	Professor of Education at the Department of Education, University of Oxford, and a Senior Research Fellow at Jesus College, Oxford. Research focus on school effectiveness and improvement, school leadership, teaching effectiveness and professional development, and promoting equity and inclusion in education.
Aaron Bradbury	A principal lecturer in early childhood at Nottingham Trent University with specialisms in early help, child development and child protection. Blog author and co-author of *Early Childhood Theories Today*.
Ruth Swailes	A school improvement adviser, education consultant and curriculum developer. Author of several blogs and co-author of *Early Childhood Theories Today*.
Brenda Taggart	A researcher in pre-school, pedagogy, developmental psychology, longitudinal study and early childhood education.

6. Plan examples

Long-term plan example

	Term 1 Autumn 1	Term 2 Autumn 2	Term 3 Spring 1	Term 4 Spring 2	Term 5 Summer 1	Term 6 Summer 2
Theme	**All about me**	**Celebrations**	**Space**	**Amazing animals**	**Around the world**	**Dinosaurs**
Communication and language	The development of children's spoken language underpins all seven areas of learning. Children's interactions from an early age form the foundations for language development. The number and quality of the interactions that they have with adults and peers throughout the day is crucial to support communication and language development. These interactions happen in a variety of contexts, in a variety of times in the day. They may include: reading stories, fact books and poems with children; introducing and using everyday and technical vocabulary; conversations and negotiations; role play; sharing ideas; adults modelling language; and adults extending thinking through questioning. These events will happen every day in all areas of the environment.					
Key texts/books	*Pumpkin Soup* *The Rainbow Fish* *The Selfish Crocodile*	*Firework* poems *The Best Diwali Ever* *Meerkat Christmas* *The Jolly Christmas Postman* *Little Glow* *Meerkat Mail*	*Smart Kids: Space: For Kids Who Really Love Space!* *It Was a Cold, Dark Night* *Astronaut and Rocket Ship* poem *Astro Girl* *Man on the Moon*	*The Gigantic Turnip* *Wriggle and Roar* *Dear Zoo* *What the Ladybird Heard* *Farmer Duck* *Jack and the Beanstalk*	*Handa's Surprise* *Percy's Bumpy Ride* *Percy the Park Keeper* stories *Mr Gumpy's Outing*	*Dear Dinosaur* *Harry and the Bucketful of Dinosaurs* *Stomp, Dinosaur Stomp!* *The Dinosaur*
	Daily phonics, following scheme					

	Term 1 Autumn 1	Term 2 Autumn 2	Term 3 Spring 1	Term 4 Spring 2	Term 5 Summer 1	Term 6 Summer 2
Personal, social and emotional development	**All about me** Name and identify feelings. To know why it is important to be kind and gentle. To know my rights and responsibilities in the classroom. **Books:** *The Lion Inside* *Milo's Monster* *The Day the Crayons Quit* *Grumpy Bird*	**Same and different** To know that being different is okay and makes life interesting. To identify ways we are different and the same. To know what a friend does and doesn't do. To know words and actions to be assertive. **Books:** *Elmer* *Barry the Fish with Fingers* *The Family Book* *The Dog and the Dolphin*	**Aspirations** Understand what perseverance is and that not giving up is how we learn. To be able to talk about a goal and how to work towards it. To know how to support my friends and classmates. To be able to celebrate my achievements and say what I am good at. **Books**: Love Monster series *Don't Worry, Hugless Douglas*	**Being healthy** To know why exercise is important. To know why sleep and rest are important. To know that some foods are healthy and some unhealthy. To know why and when to wash hands. To know that not all people are kind and how to keep safe with strangers. **Books:** *Never Talk to Strangers* *Not Everyone is Nice* *Perfectly Norman*	**Relationships** To know why being kind is important. To know what to do if I want to say sorry to someone. To know how to calm down if I am angry. To know what a good friend is. **Books:** *Incredible You* *Only One You* *I'm Sticking with You*	**Growing up** To be able to name general parts of the human body using correct names. To know how people grow from a baby to an elderly person. To begin transition to Year 1 and to use vocabulary that expresses excitement and nerves. To share memories and see how the children have grown throughout the year.

	Term 1 Autumn 1	Term 2 Autumn 2	Term 3 Spring 1	Term 4 Spring 2	Term 5 Summer 1	Term 6 Summer 2
						Books: *I Wonder Why Kangaroos Have Pouches* *The Huge Bag of Worries* *Look Inside your Body*
Physical development	**Cooperation and moving**	**Ball skills and wheeled toys**	**Ball skills and moving to music**	**Balance**	**Obstacles**	**Team games**
	Gross motor: Develop good personal hygiene – flush toilet and wash hands Cooperation games, i.e. parachute Safely climbing on outdoor play frame	**Gross motor:** Ball skills – throwing and catching Skipping ropes Dance-related activities Balance bikes, pedal bikes and trikes	**Gross motor:** Ball skills – aiming, dribbling, pushing, throwing and catching, patting, or kicking Gymnastics and balance activities Using a variety of objects in different ways, e.g. hoops, ropes, beanbags	**Gross motor:** Gymnastics and dance – focus on learning to spin, rock, tilt, fall and slide Learn different patterns of locomotion – skip, hop, run backwards, crawl, roll	**Gross motor:** Learn to navigate obstacles – moving over, under, through and around equipment Begin games that require foot-to-eye and hand-to-eye coordination – football, bats, balls	**Gross motor:** Races / team games involving speed and changing of direction Learn games for sports day, e.g. running race, beanbag throw, javelin throw

	Term 1 Autumn 1	Term 2 Autumn 2	Term 3 Spring 1	Term 4 Spring 2	Term 5 Summer 1	Term 6 Summer 2
	Fine motor: Pencil grip; encourage tripod grip Dough – developing whole-hand muscles Name writing Threading, cutting, weaving Finger gym Draw lines and circles Hold pencil/paint brush beyond whole-hand grasp	**Fine motor:** Daily name/ consonant-vowel-consonant (CVC) writing activities Threading, cutting, weaving, playdough Handwriting – teach and model correct letter formation	**Fine motor:** CVC writing activities Threading, cutting, weaving, playdough Handwriting – begin to form letters correctly Tinker table – handle tools, objects	**Fine motor:** CVC writing activities Threading, cutting, weaving, playdough Handwriting – form recognisable letters, most correctly formed Use one hand consistently for fine motor tasks Start to colour inside the lines of a picture	**Fine motor:** Sentence writing activities Threading, cutting, weaving, playdough Handwriting – form recognisable letters, most correctly formed Cut along a straight and curved line with scissors / start to cut along a curved line, like a circle / draw a cross	**Fine motor:** Threading, cutting, weaving, playdough Handwriting – form letters correctly Begin to draw diagonal lines Use a range of small tools, including scissors, paint brushes and cutlery

	Term 1 Autumn 1	Term 2 Autumn 2	Term 3 Spring 1	Term 4 Spring 2	Term 5 Summer 1	Term 6 Summer 2
Maths	Recognise numerals to 10; write numerals to 10; count to 10; composition of numbers to 5; subitising to 5; number bonds to 5; recognise and explore 2D and 3D shapes	Recognise numerals to 20; write numerals to 20; count to 20; composition of numbers to 10; one more / one less; sharing numbers; repeating patterns	Number bonds to 10; composition of numbers to 20; comparing quantities; sharing; odd and even numbers	Explore 2D and 3D shapes using informal and mathematical language; select, rotate and manipulate shapes in order to develop spatial reasoning skills	Counting in 2s; addition and subtraction; doubling/ halving; select manipulatives to solve a given problem	Numbers beyond 20; counting in 2s, 5s and 10s; addition and subtraction beyond 20; problem-solving
Understanding the world	Children will make sense of the world around them. This will be done through local visits (park, library, post box, museum, town centre). They will listen to visitors talk about their jobs, their lives and their interests. They will meet a variety of people with different jobs, such as police officers, nurses and firefighters. Children will listen to a broad selection of stories, facts, rhymes and poems offering a variety of topics including moments in time, diversity, cultures and family dimensions. Children will explore different environments and areas of the school such as the woodlands, computer suite and library.					
	To become familiar with the school and to navigate the classroom and outdoor space with confidence.	Explore different ways of celebrating Christmas in different homes and in different countries.	Introduce the children to recycling and how it can take care of our world. Look at what rubbish can do to our environment.	To know a habitat is an animal's natural home. Know animal names and the names of their young.	Past and present shops, linked to *The Tiger Who Came to Tea*, including milkman, greengrocer, butcher, baker.	To understand where dinosaurs are now and begin to understand that they were alive a very long time ago.

	Term 1 Autumn 1	Term 2 Autumn 2	Term 3 Spring 1	Term 4 Spring 2	Term 5 Summer 1	Term 6 Summer 2
	Understanding my family or relationships that are important to me. To talk through shared experiences with family, such as holidays and special occasions. Listen to other people's family experiences and draw similarities and identify differences. Read stories about different types of families and cultures around the world. Can name five senses.	Show photos of how Christmas used to be celebrated in the past. Use world maps to show children where some stories are based. Talk about and look at different types of celebrations for different religions and in a variety of cultures. Observe seasonal changes, e.g. autumn leaves, freezing ice and frost, rain.	Talk about space junk and old satellites. Look at 3D models of the planets. Try and learn their names and different features of each planet. Look at the history of space exploration. Know the sun is a star, made of burning gas.	Compare animals from a jungle to those that live in the ocean. Explore a range of jungle animals and sea creatures. Learn their names and label their habitats. Explore the lifecycle of a frog and other living things.	After close observation, draw pictures of the natural world, including animals and plants. Use Bee-Bots on simple maps. Encourage the children to use navigational language. Caring for animals in the environment, making bird feeders and encouraging children to care for the environment.	To begin to develop the concept of a timeline and different times in history. Learn about what a palaeontologist is and how they learn about dinosaurs by looking at fossils. Introduce Mary Anning as the first female to find a fossil. Classify dinosaurs based on diet and appearance. To understand that dinosaurs came from eggs and name other animals we know that come from eggs.

	Term 1 Autumn 1	Term 2 Autumn 2	Term 3 Spring 1	Term 4 Spring 2	Term 5 Summer 1	Term 6 Summer 2
		Local walk linked to *Jolly Postman* and posting letters to Santa, discussing what we will see on our journey to the post box and how we will get there.				
Expressive Arts and Design (EAD)	Children will be provided with a variety of EAD experiences every day within the continuous provision and daily routine. Some examples of this are daily singing, musical instruments, recorded music, dance and performance stage, paint, junk modelling, cutting and sticking.					
	Self portraits Using the materials in CP area correctly Autumn collages Mixing colours Harvest songs Exploring body percussion	Firework pictures (using glitter as a highlight) Making rocket models Making Christmas decorations and cards Making Divas Christmas songs and nativity	Winter pictures Making some space music Making shadow puppets	Flower collages Rousseau's Tiger / animal prints	African art and music Aboriginal art and music Making scarecrows and other items to protect the seeds Vegetable printing (repeated patterns)	Making model dinosaurs from clay

Medium-term plan example: Personal, Social and Emotional Development (PSED)

Being Healthy: Term 5

Week	Learning objective	Possible activities and enhancements	Key questions and vocab
1	To know why we should exercise.	• Feel our hearts before and after exercise. • Listen to our hearts with the stethoscope. • Write a fitness diary listing the exercise we do each day. • Learn a variety of different exercises and describe how they keep us fit, e.g. running for heart and lungs, push-ups and sit-ups to develop strength. • Have a visiting sportsperson or PE teacher in to talk through how and why they keep fit. • Watch fitness videos by Joe Wicks and join in. • Talk about why we need to keep drinking water, especially after exercise. • Fuzzy felt body parts puzzle. • Book display: *Yoga Pretzels*; *My Book of Gymnastics*; *Football*; *Karate for Kids*	How does our heart feel different before and after exercise? What does our heart do? What do our lungs do? What do our muscles do? Why do we puff when we exercise? How can our bodies change with exercise? **Vocabulary**: health, fitness, heart, lungs, wellbeing

Week	Learning objective	Possible activities and enhancements	Key questions and vocab
2	To know why sleep is important.	• Talk through the routine of getting to bed – bath, brush teeth, story, PJs, bed, lights out, etc. Explore if everyone has the same bedtime routine. • Add bed and cot to home corner and PJs for teddies and dolls. • Talk about sleep – how we feel well rested, how we feel tired. Discuss effect on concentration and mood when have not slept enough. • Draw two pictures of yourself, one when you have had enough sleep, one when you are tired. What is the difference? • Talk about animals sleeping and look at pictures, e.g. where do fish sleep? Where do mice sleep? Talk about every animal needing to sleep. • Learn some bedtime songs, such as lullabies.	Why do we yawn? What do you need to help you sleep well? How do you feel if you don't sleep? **Vocabulary**: sleep, rest, tired, concentration, health

Week	Learning objective	Possible activities and enhancements	Key questions and vocab
3	To know some healthy and unhealthy foods.	• Sorting activity – food and two hoops: healthy food and treat food (less healthy) • Make a healthy plate – stick pictures onto a paper plate. • Make some healthy snacks – cut up cucumber sticks, make smoothies, make cheese sandwich. • Enhancement – unusual fruits and vegetables – can you name them? • Fruit tasting – try some new fruits, such as pineapple, mango, lychee, etc. • Make a whole-class bar chart of our favourite vegetable.	How often should you eat sweets in a week? What happens to your body if you eat too many treat foods in a week? **Vocabulary**: healthy, treat, unhealthy, sugar, fats
4	To know unhealthy foods may be bad for our teeth.	• Look at the big toothbrush and teeth. Talk about how we clean our teeth. Leave it out as an enhancement. • Learn the *Brush Your Teeth* song. • Make a dentist role play alongside the home corner. • Look at the sequence of brushing teeth. Children practise with actions as you go through it. Display the sequence. • Laminated teeth picture and toothbrush – brush off the muck (made with whiteboard pen).	What will happen if you don't brush your teeth? How often should you brush your teeth? Have you ever been to the dentist? What did they do? **Vocabulary**: teeth, tooth, toothbrush, decay, plaque, filling, dentist

Week	Learning objective	Possible activities and enhancements	Key questions and vocab
5	To know why handwashing helps us stay healthy.	• Learn a song about handwashing. • Experiment – children handle slices of bread with clean hands and dirty hands. Put the bread in bags and watch the changes as the bread gets older. • Look at 'How to wash your hands' poster. Go through each step. Put up by sinks for children to copy. • Look at images of microbes under a microscope. Talk about why they look different and why we can't see them normally. Leave some microscopes out in provision.	Why is it important to wash your hands? What are bacteria? How long should you wash your hands for? Why do we use soap to wash our hands? **Vocabulary**: soap, handwashing, bacteria, germs, virus, scrub, water, microbes

Medium-term plan example: Understanding the World (UW)

Animals: Term 4

Week	Learning objective	Possible activities and enhancements	Key questions and vocab
1	To know a habitat is an animal's natural home.	• Look at some images of different habitats. Identify different features of each habitat. • Match picture cards of animals to their habitats. • Create a habitat in a tuff tray. Ask children to choose the correct small-world animals to put in the habitat.	Is a zoo a habitat? Why do animals prefer certain habitats? Can humans live in every type of habitat? **Vocabulary**: habitat, grassland, sea, woodland, rainforest, environment, mountain, desert

Week	Learning objective	Possible activities and enhancements	Key questions and vocab
2	To be able to identify and compare two habitats.	• Look at pictures and videos of the sea and the rainforest. List keywords that describe each as a comparison. • Sort small-world sea and rainforest animals into different hoops. • Make a chart of animals living in the two different habitats. Leave it on display and ask children to add to it if they think of any more later. • Paint sea and rainforest pictures. Children choose what they want to paint, but must describe the features of the habitat they have chosen. • Look at a globe and some maps. Identify some places that have rainforest, and look at the sea. Explain the sea is blue on the globe.	Is there just one sea, or several in the world and do they all have the same animals? Which countries have rainforest? What is the difference between a forest and a rainforest? Why is the globe a ball shape? **Vocabulary**: sea, ocean, water, rainforest, forest, globe, world, map, whale, dolphin, fish, monkey, snake, sloth
3	To be able to identify and compare two habitats.	• All ideas from the Week 2 lesson, but compare desert and grassland.	Is Antarctica a desert? **Vocabulary**: grassland, savannah, desert, zebra, giraffe, wildebeest, lion

Week	Learning objective	Possible activities and enhancements	Key questions and vocab
4	To identify features of one animal, e.g. frog.	• Frog and pond habitat in tuff tray. • Label parts of a frog diagram. • Make a frog from junk modelling. • Make a zip book of each of the stages of life for a frog. • Go to the pond and look for some eggs or tadpoles. Do some pond dipping. • Look at some images of different frogs and consider why they are different colours. Introduce the term 'camouflage' and ask which other animals have camouflage. Make the link between their colour and their habitat.	What does a frog eat? How does a frog get its food? What habitat does a frog live in? Do frogs have any enemies (predators)? Why do frogs jump and not walk? **Vocabulary**: head, body, tail, diet, predator, habitat, eye, tongue
5	To understand the lifecycle of a frog.	• To think about how some babies look the same as their parents (e.g. humans) while others look different (e.g. ladybirds and butterflies). Explain that they have different names. • Match images and names of adults to baby animals. • Watch the following video: The Life Cycle of a Frog | Frog Life Cycle | Science for Kids! By Twinkl education: www.youtube.com/watch?v=FEgdsLBHWAU • Make a diagram of the lifecycle of a frog – glue images in the correct order on the lifecycle (cloze activity).	Where do frogs lay their eggs? What are frogs' eggs called? What do tadpoles eat? When do frogs lay their frogspawn? **Vocabulary**: frog, amphibian, lifecycle, egg, tadpole, froglet, adult, change, grow, metamorphosis

Knowledge organiser example: Space

Key vocabulary

planet
moon
Sun
star
Earth
solar system
orbit
astronaut
space shuttle
asteroid

Did you know …

Neil Armstrong was the first person to walk on the Moon.

Key questions

Where is space?

What is a person called who travels into space?

How do they travel into space?

What do they wear?

What do you think is in outer space?

Which planet do we live on?

What could you use to see space clearly?

What planets can you name?

Key events

1949 – The first monkey is sent into space.

1955 – The 'Space Race' begins between the Soviet Union and United States of America.

1957 – The first animal orbits the Earth in space: Laika, the dog.

1961 – The first man goes into space: Yuri Gagarin.

1963 – The first woman goes into space: Valentina Tereshkova.

1969 – The first people land on the Moon.

What do we need to know about space?

Space is a long, long way up in the sky.

Astronauts travel to space in a rocket or space shuttle.

Astronauts wear special space suits with helmets and gravity boots.

There is less gravity in space than on Earth.

It is very dark in space with lots of stars.

There are different planets and other objects in space, including the Earth, the Sun and the Moon.

We live on the planet called Earth.

Here are the other planets in space:

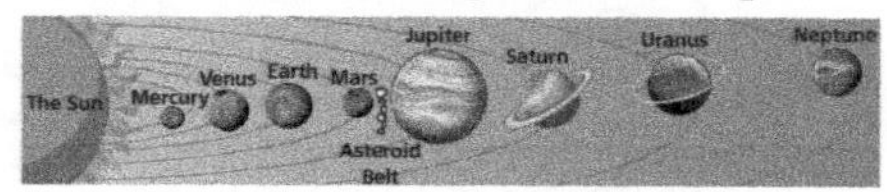

Knowledge organiser example: Minibeasts

Key vocabulary
insect

antenna

wings

habitat

lifecycle

caterpillar

shell

cocoon

chrysalis

lava

eggs

backbone

invertebrate

Key questions
What type of minibeasts do you know?

What is a lifecycle?

What is a habitat?

What are some types of habitat?

What does a caterpillar change into?

What does a tadpole change into?

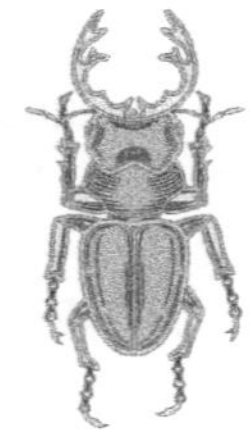

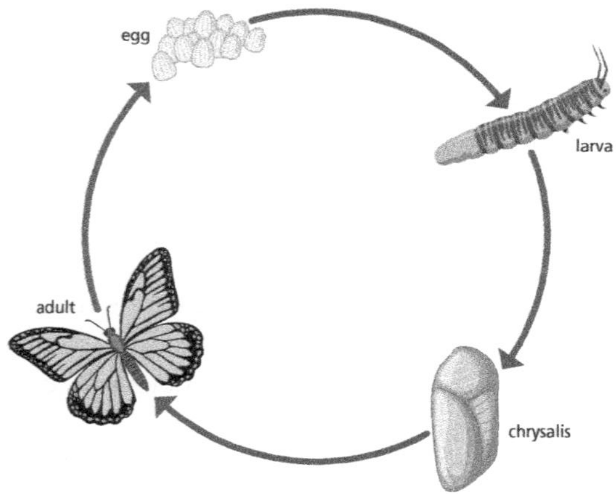

What do we need to know about minibeasts?
Minibeasts are very important for many reasons and we need to look after them.

Minibeasts do not have a backbone.

Minibeasts live in different habitats.

There are more invertebrates in the world than any other type of animal.

Sample timetable for Reception

	Monday	Tuesday	Wednesday	Thursday	Friday
8.45	Registration and morning challenge	Registration and morning challenge	Registration and morning challenge	Registration and morning challenge	Registration and morning challenge
9.00	Phonics	Phonics	Phonics	Phonics	Phonics
9.20	Continuous provision	Library and ICT sessions	Continuous provision	Continuous provision	Forest school
10.10	Tidy up and singing	Tidy up and singing	Tidy up and singing	Tidy up and singing	Tidy up and singing
10.30	Maths	English	Maths	English	Maths
10.40	Continuous provision	Continuous provision	Continuous provision	Continuous provision	Continuous provision
11.30	Toileting and rhymes	Toileting and rhymes	Toileting and rhymes	Toileting and rhymes	Toileting and rhymes
11.45	Lunch in dining hall	Lunch in dining hall	Lunch in dining hall	Lunch in dining hall	Lunch in dining hall
12.15	Playtime on big playground	Playtime on big playground	Playtime on big playground	Playtime on big playground	Playtime on big playground
12.45	Topic carpet session	PE indoors and hall time	English	Topic carpet session	Topic carpet session
1.15	Continuous provision and interventions	Continuous provision and interventions	Continuous provision and interventions	Continuous provision and interventions	Continuous provision and interventions
2.30	Tidy up	Tidy up	Tidy up	Tidy up	Tidy up
2.45	Storytime and home time	Storytime and home time	Storytime and home time	Storytime and home time	Storytime and home time

Sample timetable for nursery

	8.45	9.00	9.20	10.10	10.30	10.45	11.30	12.15	12.40	2.30	2.45	3.00
Friday	Welcome and settle	Key group time	Continuous provision and snack bar	Tidy up	Story and phonics	Continuous provision	Lunch and change of morning/afternoon children	Key group time	Continuous provision	Tidy up	Story and phonics	Home time
Thursday	Welcome and settle	Key group time	Continuous provision and snack bar	Tidy up	Story and phonics	Continuous provision	Lunch and change of morning/afternoon children	Key group time	Outdoor play with Reception class	Tidy up	Story and phonics	Home time
Wednesday	Welcome and settle	Key group time	Continuous provision and snack bar	Tidy up	Story and phonics	Outdoor play with Reception class	Lunch and change of morning/afternoon children	Key group time	Continuous provision	Tidy up	Story and phonics	Home time
Tuesday	Welcome and settle	Key group time	Continuous provision and snack bar	Tidy up	Story and phonics	Continuous provision	Lunch and change of morning/afternoon children	Key group time	Continuous provision	Tidy up	Story and phonics	Home time
Monday	Welcome and settle	Key group time	Continuous provision and snack bar	Tidy up	Story and phonics	Continuous provision	Lunch and change of morning/afternoon children	Key group time	Continuous provision	Tidy up	Story and phonics	Home time

Continuous provision and enhancements plan example: nursery

Themes, topics or skill focus: *Gruffalo* story		Week:
	Indoors	
Area	**Adult-focused learning**	**Enhancements**
Book corner	***Cur area**: CL **Obj**: Listen to longer stories and remember what happens. **Activity**: Read *The Gruffalo* – look at pictures together.	**Cur area**: CL Gruffalo toys and puppets, other books by Julia Donaldson
Construction		**Cur area**: Maths, PD, EAD LEGO®
Water tray		**Cur area**: PD Sealife small world and boats
Writing table	***Cur area**: L **Obj**: To write some letters accurately. **Activity**: Variety of character worksheets with space to write labels. Use word cards and shadow writing to support writing.	
Creative		**Cur area**: EAD, PD Watercolour paints and paper

*Focus area with an adult. Every child must do this activity at least once. Monitored by ticking off name list.

Area	Adult-focused learning	Enhancements
Round table		**Cur area**: Maths Puzzles
Small world		**Cur area**: CL Gruffalo-themed tuff tray, Gruffalo characters on lolly sticks to make puppets, resources to make the Gruffalo scene such as trees and logs
Fine motor	***Cur area**: PD **Obj**: Develop skills and coordination using tools. **Activity**: Cutting and sticking – cut out pictures of Gruffalo and other characters from the book.	
Sensory		**Cur area**: PD Shaving foam, paintbrushes and glitter
Dough		**Cur area**: EAD Air-dry clay and tools
Maths	***Cur area**: Maths **Obj**: To understand and be able to demonstrate the prepositions 'over', 'under', 'in' **Activity**: Use a small toy from the Gruffalo story and a box. Ask children to demonstrate where the toy goes for the different key words. Model for children who are unsure.	**Cur area**: Maths Leave activity out for children to redo if they wish

Area	Adult-focused learning	Enhancements
Investigation		**Cur area**: UW Light table with colour overlays
Home corner		**Cur area**: UW, CL Normal set up with addition of baby and cot
	Outdoors	
Sand		**Cur area**: PD, CL Buckets and spades
Water		**Cur area**: PD Large gutters and trays, jugs and cups
Performance area	***Cur area**: CL, L – reading **Obj**: To be able to re-enact parts of a well-known story. **Activity**: Put on masks and costumes and re-enact parts of the story, e.g. when the different characters meet. Use some key phrases, such as, 'Who is this creature with terrible claws…'.	
Large physical	***Cur area**: PD **Obj**: Skip, hop, stand on one leg. **Activity**: Teach children how to play hopscotch.	
Mud kitchen		**Cur area**: CL Make a stew for the Gruffalo's dinner using pots, soil, water, leaves, spoons, bowls, bark, twigs

Area	Adult-focused learning	Enhancements
Large construction		**Cur area**: Maths, PD, CL Den making
Tinker table		**Cur area**: PD Saws and hammers
Asphalt area	See *Large physical* – hopscotch	
Maths	See *Large physical* – hopscotch	
Creative	*__Cur area__: EAD **Obj**: To explore different textures and to use imagination for what to do with them. **Activity**: Make large collage of Gruffalo to display.	
Nature	*__Cur area__: UW **Obj**: Use all their senses in hands-on exploration of natural materials. **Activity**: Planting sunflowers. **Resources**: Set of laminated instructions for how to plant a sunflower, pots, seeds, compost, labels and pens.	
Mark making		**Cur area**: L Whiteboards, paper, pencils, pens, envelopes, Gruffalo colouring sheets.

Continuous provision and enhancements plan example: Reception

Themes, topics or skill focus: Once Upon a Time (Cinderella week)		Week:
	Indoors	
Area	**Adult-focused learning**	**Enhancements**
Book corner		**Cur area**: Literacy (reading) Fairy tale books: *Cinderella*; *The Three Little Pigs*; *Snow White* Fairytale characters, character puppets and soft toys
Construction	***Cur area**: Maths **Obj**: To correctly name the 3D shapes cube, cone and cylinder. **Activity**: To build Cinderella's castle out of wooden blocks.	
Water tray		**Cur area**: PD (fine motor control) Variety of jugs and containers, and wheel spinners
Writing table	***Cur area**: Literacy (writing) **Obj**: To write a letter and address an envelope. **Activity**: Write an invitation to the ball. Address an envelope and put the invitation inside.	

*Focus area with an adult. Every child must do this activity at least once. Monitored by ticking off name list.

Area	Adult-focused learning	Enhancements
Creative area	***Cur area**: EAD **Obj**: Join different materials and explore different textures. **Activity**: Make a dress for Cinderella to wear to the ball.	
Round table		**Cur area**: CL Finger puppets or Cinderella characters
Small world		**Cur area:** UW, CL Small-world dolls and carriage playset
Fine motor		**Cur area**: PD, EAD Threading ribbon on small loom frames
Sensory		**Cur area**: PD, UW Coloured cornflour gloop on tuff tray with tools that scrape
Dough		**Cur area**: PD (hand strength) Salt dough
Maths	*See construction for maths focus task*	
Investigation		**Cur area**: UW Battery sets, wires with clips and bulbs, switches, simple circuit diagrams

Area	Adult-focused learning	Enhancements
Home corner		**Cur area**: PSED, CL Add to home corner: broom, mop, mixing bowl, rolling pin, sifter, dry rice and pasta, teapot. Remove babies and cot.
Carpet area		**Cur area**: M Polydron sets
	Outdoors	
Sand	*__Cur area__: PD and UW **Obj**: To understand a metal detector sends an electromagnetic field to the ground that attracts metal. **Activity**: Find the treasure – use the handheld metal detector to find hidden coins in the sand.	**Cur area**: UW Tuff tray with a variety of objects made from different materials. Put pots for children to sort into material groupings – metal, wood, plastic, fabric.
Water		**Cur area**: EAD Making potions and mixing colours. Containers of different-coloured water, droppers, small jars.
Performance area		**Cur area**: EAD Use props to re-enact the Cinderella story: princess dresses, high-heeled shoes, pumpkin, toy mice, broom, dressing-up suits, Cinderella story to read through.

Area	Adult-focused learning	Enhancements
Large physical	*See asphalt area*	
Mud kitchen		**Cur area**: PD, CL Water, mud, pots, pans, kitchen
Large construction		**Cur area**: Maths, PD Crates and large planks
Large table		**Cur area**: Maths, PD Extension tasks (completing missing numbers on laminated number tracks 0–10), whiteboard pens
Tinker table		**Cur area**: PD, EAD Hammers, nails, wood, plastic bottle tops, safety glasses, vice
Asphalt area		**Cur area**: PD Balance cans, hoops, skipping ropes
Creative	***Cur area**: EAD **Obj**: Develop own ideas and decide which materials to use to express them. Join different materials and explore different textures. **Activity**: Make a carriage for Cinderella from junk modelling.	

Area	Adult-focused learning	Enhancements
Nature		**Cur area**: UW Assorted-sized pine cones and pebbles, magnifying glasses. Add books on trees and science cards (laminated) on types of pines.
Maths	***Cur area**: Maths (sequencing), Literacy (reading) **Obj**: To be able to sequence three or more parts of a story correctly. **Activity**: Put six picture story cards in order. Encourage children to talk through each picture and explain the sequence. To be done with a partner of differing ability to encourage partner talk.	
Mark making		**Cur area**: L (writing) Variety of small booklets and a variety of pens the children haven't used before, e.g. glitter pens

Weekly planning: Maths

Date:

<table>
<tr><th>Objectives</th><th>Main teaching</th><th>Group work and enhancements</th><th>Resources</th><th>Questions and vocabulary</th></tr>
<tr><td rowspan="3">To recognise numerals 0–10 and to count them in order.
Link numerals to their amounts 0–10.
To know we can count things we can't see.</td><td>Day: Tuesday
Sing some counting songs: Once I Caught a Fish Alive; One, Two, Buckle My Shoe.
Show the die (number, not dots) and talk through how it works by rolling. Top number being the number you use. Identify each number.
Show the snakes and ladders board. Model how to play the game. Tell children they are going to have a go playing it in groups.</td><td rowspan="3">Group: Play snakes and ladders. Two children and one adult per group.
Group: 1:1 – have digit cards 1–10 out on table. Ask child to put the correct number of buttons on each card to match quantity to digit.
Enhancements:
Book corner: number book display
• books: Ten Little Ladybugs; One Mole Digging a Hole; Ten Black Dots
• gel digits
• numicon
• shells
• cubes.
Writing table: number tracks 0–10 with missing digits – laminated alongside whiteboard pens.
Outside: chalk and sets of large digits to copy onto pavement.
Washing line: digit cards 0–10 in the wrong order. Can they be put in the correct order.</td><td rowspan="3">Snakes and ladders board
Number die
Sets of digit cards (small and large)
Number books
Gel digits
Numicon
Shells
Cubes
Chalk
Washing line and pegs</td><td rowspan="3">How many altogether?
What comes after …?
What mistake have I made?
Can you count?
Is this in the right order?
Why does the order matter?
Vocabulary: number names, count, order, place, die, how many, digit</td></tr>
<tr><td>Day: Thursday
Sing some counting songs: Five Little Speckled Frogs; Five Fat Sausages.
Have digit cards and items and model how to match quantities. Occasionally make an error and ask the children to call out when it is wrong.
Play speed flash – hold up a digit card to 5 and children quickly hold up that many fingers.</td></tr>
<tr><td>Day: Friday
Sing some counting songs: Five Little Men in a Flying Saucer, Five Little Monkeys Jumping on the Bed.
Explain we can count things we can't see – give examples, e.g. claps, beats on the drum, clicks. Tell children to close their eyes and listen to a set of claps. Count and hold up fingers for the amount of claps you can hear. Play a few times. Give out whiteboards. Play the same game but ask children to write the digit of the number of claps they heard.</td></tr>
</table>

Weekly planning: Literacy

Date:

Objectives	Main teaching	Group work and enhancements	Resources	Questions and vocabulary
To know the differences between fiction and fact books. To know what labels are used for in fact books. To be able to express an opinion about a book.	**Day:** Tuesday Have a fiction and fact book (*The Very Hungry Caterpillar* and *The Lifecycle of a Butterfly*). Ask children to look at the cover of both. What do the covers tell us about the books? What do we think they will be about? They both have images of caterpillars, so will they be about the same thing? What clues does the cover give us about the type of book we are going to read? Introduce the vocabulary fiction and fact. Tell the children which book is fiction and say you can tell this by the illustration and the title. Read the fiction story and tell the children that tomorrow we will read the fact book.	**Group:** Read some fact books in a small group. **Enhancement:** Put two empty baskets in book corner labelled 'fiction' and 'fact'. Encourage children to sort some books into them.	Selection of fiction and fact books Hoop Fiction/ fact labels Caterpillar diagram and labels Glue	Can a fiction book have labels? What is a fact? What is a label for? **Vocabulary:** fact, fiction, illustration, drawing, title, label, parts
	Day: Wednesday Remind children of the words fiction and fact. Get them to explain again the difference between the two books. Read the fact book about caterpillars to the children. After reading it, turn back to some pages and look at the features in more detail including the title and labels. Have children discuss the features of fact and fiction books and write their ideas on large paper to put on the working wall.	**Group:** Refer to the book to label the picture of the caterpillar by gluing correct word in the correct space. **Enhancement:** Writing table: blank labels (sticky notes). Encourage children to label things around the classroom.		
	Day: Thursday Remind children about what we learned about fiction and fact books. Have two hoops on the floor with the label fiction and fact. Tell children they are going to help you sort them. Hold up each book. Lead the discussion about what type of book it is and how do they know. Encourage well-formed sentences with clear justification for the choice.	**Group:** Sort a pile of books into fiction and fact hoops. Explain how they know where each book goes (repeat the whole-class activity in small groups, supporting the discussion around book types).		

Weekly planning: Topic work

Dinosaurs

Date:

<table>
<tr><th>Objectives</th><th>Main teaching</th><th>Group work and enhancements</th><th>Resources</th><th>Key questions and vocab</th></tr>
<tr><td rowspan="3">To know dinosaurs lived a long time ago, and they are now extinct.
To be able to identify some dinosaurs by their features.
To be able to group dinosaurs into herbivores and carnivores.</td><td>Day: Monday
Look at some pages from the fact book on dinosaurs (First Encyclopaedia of Dinosaurs). Look at some of the features of each dinosaur, such as spines, neck length, legs and teeth. Ask children why some have sharp teeth and others blunt. Introduce the vocabulary ‘carnivore’ and ‘herbivore’. Look at more dinosaurs and decide which group they are going into.
Model how to make the zip book.</td><td rowspan="3">Group:
Create a zip book of dinosaurs: four pages of herbivores and on the other side four pages of carnivores. Children choose the picture they want to stick in and have to describe which group it belongs to, and how they know.
Enhancements:
Red table: colouring sheets of different dinosaurs.
Water tray: make a dinosaur swamp.
Sand tray: Use brushes to get fossils out of sand tray.
Main screen or PCs: Andy’s Dinosaur Adventure videos (CBeebies).
Writing table outside: zip books and pictures of dinosaurs (as for group work but children can do another one independently).</td><td rowspan="3">Images of dinosaurs cut out (for zip book)
Pre-folded zip books
Dinosaur colouring sheets
Dinosaur figures
Foliage for swamp
Fossils and brushes
Dinosaur books</td><td rowspan="3">What is a herbivore?
What is a carnivore?
What do dinosaur teeth tell us?
What sort of habitat did this dinosaur live in?
What are the spines for?
What did this dinosaur eat?
Are flying dinosaurs birds?
What does cold blooded mean?
Vocabulary: extinct, pre-historic, eggs, camouflage, fossil, swamp, teeth, carnivore, herbivore</td></tr>
<tr><td>Day: Wednesday
Watch a video about dinosaurs (Diplodocus and T-rex): www.bbc.co.uk/cbeebies/curations/dinosaur-facts
Remind children of the vocabulary herbivore and carnivore. What do they think Diplodocus and T-rex were and how do they know?
Introduce the word ‘extinct’. Ask children what it means. Ask why they think the dinosaurs became extinct.
Look at some pages from the dinosaur encyclopaedia together.</td></tr>
<tr><td>Day: Friday
Watch a video about dinosaurs (Stegosaurus and Ornithocheirus): www.bbc.co.uk/cbeebies/curations/dinosaur-facts
Learn the dinosaur song: www.youtube.com/watch?v=W0FOZ0-VpcU
Do the Dinosaur Stomp dance: www.youtube.com/watch?v=IwvpvkdDeGw</td></tr>
</table>